Accelerators in Silicon Valley: Building Successful Startups

T0319621

Accelerators in Silicon Valley: Building Successful Startups

Searching for the Next Big Thing

Peter Ester

Amsterdam University Press

This research was made possible by a grant from the Dutch Van Spaendonck Foundation.

Cover design: Klaas Wijnberg
Typesetting: Crius Group, Hulshout

Amsterdam University Press English-language titles are distributed in the US and Canada by the University of Chicago Press.

ISBN	978 94 6298 716 6
e-ISBN	978 90 4853 868 3
NUR	800
DOI	10.5117/9789462987166

© P. Ester / Amsterdam University Press B.V., Amsterdam 2017

You should start with the problem that you're trying to solve in the world and not start with deciding that you want to build a company.
Mark Zuckerberg, Facebook

To all startups that contribute to a better society through their passion,
ambition, and entrepreneurship

Table of Contents

Foreword

Peter Ester brilliantly captures the varied but vital role that accelerators play in minting new entrepreneurs essential for economic development and new job creation in America. Based upon recommendations from various people, myself included, Peter set out on a mission to thoroughly study two dozen accelerators in Silicon Valley, the mecca of innovation. He chose the interview method with carefully defined questions in a quest to contrast his discoveries in Silicon Valley with Europe.

In an easy-to-read-and-grasp style of writing, Peter does an excellent job of communicating his findings. His conclusions are descriptive and prescriptive. The target readers – whether established entrepreneurs or aspiring ones and policymakers or concerned citizens imagining new ways of economic development – are in for a treat here.

Peter highlights the notion of 'culture' rather prominently in his analysis of critical success factors in Silicon Valley. He goes on to suggest that culture – which includes a winning mindset and the ability to take risks, try, and fail without a stigma being attached in European society– is an essential ingredient for success. What is common to all effective accelerators, Peter notes, is the existence of an ecosystem of successful role models and mentors who are eager to offer advice and guidance to new entrepreneurs, something that is lacking in Europe. The prevalence of investors – both angels and venture capitalists – who are willing to take risks on unproven entrepreneurs is another key ingredient in Silicon Valley that is also missing in European society.

I strongly encourage all success-seeking Europeans to pay close attention to what Peter Ester, a European, has to say in this book. This includes developing a mindset of risk-taking that is free from stigma, stepping forward to coach and mentor others, and setting up more angels and venture capital funds.

Lastly, I encourage readers to study more of Silicon Valley's successes to build better European innovations, which in turn should lead to increased economic activity, more jobs and wealth creation, and, ultimately, better societies.

Silicon Valley has stood the test of time, so it's a very safe bet to emulate a piece of it!

Vish Mishra
Venture capitalist, Clearstone Venture Partners
Accelerator advisor and startup mentor
Former president of TiE Silicon Valley

Acknowledgements

I would like to thank the founders and chief executives of the 23 Silicon Valley accelerators whom I interviewed for this study. They generously took the time to talk to me about their passion for bringing talented startups to the marketplace and to co-create new innovative businesses that may make a difference. They all share the same ambition, enthusiasm, and vision to help startups to realize their business ideas and their dreams and to grow their new venture. It was a delight to interview such able and dedicated entrepreneurs. I learned a lot about how accelerators in Silicon Valley select and foster new startups, how they empower startup teams, how they coach startups in developing their product and in sharpening their marketing strategy, and how they prepare them for entering the competition. My gratitude goes out to Saeed Amidi (Plug and Play), Sunil Bhargava (Tandem), Gary Coover (Samsung NEXT Start), Danielle D'Agostaro (Alchemist Accelerator), Doug Davenport (Prospect Silicon Valley), Cyril Ebersweiler (HAX), Marlon Evans (GSVlabs), Tom Ferguson and Nimesh Modak (Imagine H_2O), Ian Foraker (Cleantech Open), Brian Hoffman (StartX), Ari Horie (Women's Startup Lab), Emily Kirsch (Powerhouse), Cindy Klein-Marmer (Butler Venture Accelerator), Naomi Kokubo (Founders Space), Duncan Logan (RocketSpace), T.M. Ravi (The Hive), Prashant Shah (TiE LaunchPad), Prem Talreja (The Fabric), Harm TenHoff (BayLink), Marco ten Vaanholt (BootUP), Matt Walters (Runway), Jun Wong (Hacker Dojo), and Elizabeth Yin (500 Startups).

I am greatly indebted to my good friend Vish Mishra, a successful Silicon Valley entrepreneur and prominent venture capitalist, for introducing me to several accelerators and for writing the foreword to this book. The San Jose Mercury News has described Vish Mishra as one of the ten most influential people in Silicon Valley.

Peter Laanen, an equally good friend, was gracious enough to open up his accelerator network in the Bay Area to me. The Dutch Consulate in San Francisco was helpful in various phases of my research, as they had been in my previous projects on Silicon Valley's remarkable innovation track record.

I am grateful to a number of outstanding experts on Silicon Valley whom I interviewed on the vibrant Bay Area accelerator scene and its broader economic and technological impact. They include Aiaz Kazi (Head of Platform Ecosystem at Google and startup advisor), Susan Lucas-Conwell (innovation catalyst and accelerator mentor), and Sean Randolph (Senior Director of the Bay Area Council Economic Institute). I am also grateful to Anuradha Basu, Director of the Silicon Valley Center for Entrepreneurship at San Jose State University, for her insights into how the Silicon Valley ecosystem works to build successful businesses.

I want to thank Guy Bauwen and Arjen van Klink, respectively the previous and current director of the Research Center Business Innovation of Rotterdam University for Applied Sciences, for supporting this study. I greatly value the discussions on the dynamics of the startup (and scale-up) economy with my colleagues Ron Ainsbury, Guy Bauwen, Leo Klienbannink, Maaike Lycklama à Nijeholt, and Arie de Wild, and with Rotterdam Business School lecturers Peter Anker, Frits Berkhout, Rengenier Rittersma, and Bert Vermeulen. They all share a fascination with the role of startups in boosting innovation and growth.

Tim van Duren, my research associate, had a significant input as well. His accuracy was highly valuable in logistically complex projects such as this one. Jan de Kok did an excellent job of acquiring background information on the accelerators that were interviewed for this study. I have much respect for Flatworld Solutions (Bangalore, India) for making professional transcripts of the interviews I held.

Many thanks to Amelia Román, Professor of Entrepreneurship, for her professional English language correction of the manuscript and for helping me to understand Silicon Valley. I am indebted to my colleague Ron Ainsbury for his critical reading of this text, his helpful comments, and his humor. I also owe a great deal to Rengenier Rittersma, lecturer and researcher at Rotterdam Business School, for his careful examination of the manuscript.

I would like to thank Arne Maas, my friend and former colleague at the Research Center Business Innovation and co-author of my previous book *Silicon Valley: Planet Startup. Disruptive Innovation, Passionate Entrepreneurship & Hightech Startups* (Amsterdam University Press, 2016). Arne was so taken by the energetic startup culture in Silicon Valley that he decided to quit his academic career and found his own new venture (https://www.soundies.eu). Best of luck, Arne!

This research on accelerators in Silicon Valley is part of a larger study that also includes Dutch and other European accelerators. The parallel study is conducted by co-principal researcher Ferry Koster (ICOON/TIAS, Tilburg University) and his research associate Merijn Bernat. It was a pleasure working with Ferry and Merijn: our cooperation based on scientific curiosity, i.e., the need to understand and explain, has been an unbeatable asset.

Many thanks to Gioia Marini, Maryse Elliott, Chantal Nicolaes, and Thijs Borgers of Amsterdam University Press for their professional guidance of every phase of this book project. It was a pleasure working with you.

Finally, I want to express my gratitude to the Dutch Van Spaendonck Foundation for commissioning this study. I cherish the Board discussions on innovation and entrepreneurship I had with Hans Kamps, Dick van der Laan, and Carmen de Jonge, as well as with Jan Gevers, CEO of Van Spaendonck, on the role of startup accelerators in the new economy.

I sincerely hope that the conclusions from this study will help to advance a pro-accelerator climate in the Netherlands and in the rest of Europe. In order to remain economically and technologically competitive, Europe must substantially invest in building a dynamic and entrepreneurial startup ecosystem. As Silicon Valley demonstrates, accelerators play a distinctive role in taking (and retaining) the lead in the global innovation arena.

Peter Ester
Rotterdam/Silicon Valley, Summer 2017

The Interviewees and their Accelerators

Below, I provide brief descriptions of the people I interviewed and the accelerators they lead.

Saeed Amidi, founder and CEO of Plug and Play, a large accelerator housing nearly 400 startups, with 22 locations worldwide. Plug and Play has accelerated over 2,000 startups, which have raised an additional $5 billion. It invests anywhere from $25,000 up to $500,000 in its startups. Offers different industry-specific, three-month accelerator programs (in brand and retail, financial technology, food, health, insurance, Internet of Things, mobility, new materials, logistics, travel and hospitality). Plug and Play may take equity in its startups.

Sunil Bhargava, founder and managing partner of Tandem, a seed fund. Small accelerator for hardware and software startups. Its focus is on mobile. Investing both sweat and financial capital. The current fund, Tandem 3, is $100 million in size. Tandem offers a six-month program in which it works hands-on with portfolio companies to find product-market fit. Investments in early-stage seed deals up to $500,000 and later-stage investments up to $2 million; it may take about 10% equity in its startups. Small batches: two to six teams. It currently has investments in over 30 companies.

Gary Coover, head of global operations at Samsung NEXT Start, a corporate accelerator. It invests in seed-stage startups and entrepreneurs-in-residence who it supports in co-located spaces with funding, expertise, mentoring, and an alumni community. Its focus is on software startups (both consumer and enterprise-oriented) in frontier technology such as AR/VR, IoT, mobility, data and analytics, machine learning and AI, mobile health, payments, and smart cities.

Danielle D'Agostaro, partner and COO at Alchemist Accelerator, a venture-backed general accelerator focusing on growing seed-stage enterprise startups. Alchemist seeds about 40 startups per year with an average cash investment of $36,000. Co-working space is available. Strong emphasis on technical founding teams. The length of the accelerator program is six months, and it accepts a maximum of 17 teams in three batches per year. Its program consists of mentoring, coaching, and group activities. The average equity required is around 5%.

Doug Davenport, founder and former CEO of Prospect Silicon Valley, a non-profit urban-tech innovation hub for next-generation smart and sustainable cities. Its focus is on transportation, energy, and the built environment. Prospect works with industry and government. It helps startups to demonstrate and commercialize their products and scale their companies. It has a 23,000 square-foot Technology Demonstration Center, over 25 corporate sponsors, and over $90 million funding and financing. It takes no equity in its startups.

Cyril Ebersweiler, founder and managing director of HAX, an investment company that accelerates hardware startups – both consumer hardware and B2B. Its focus is on lifestyle, health, robotics, Internet of Things, and manufacturing. Provides seed funding, mentorship, office and lab space. Selected teams spend 15 weeks of the four-month program in Shenzhen, China – the 'Silicon Valley of hardware' – to finalize their prototype. HAX accepts two classes per year and 15 teams per class. Equity is 9% for $100,000.

Marlon Evans, CEO of GSVlabs, a large 72,000 square-foot campus and co-working space that provides a community for startups and established companies who wish to accelerate their vision. Its focus is on education technology (EdTech), sustainability, big data, and mobility. It is backed by GSV Capital. GSVlabs offers virtual and onsite programs, innovation labs, mentorship, and events. It currently houses about 170 startups. Startups pay a monthly desk fee. GSVlabs does not make direct investments, but it does take equity in startups participating in its quarterly accelerator.

Tom Ferguson and Nimesh Modak are respectively vice president of programming and director of Imagine H$_2$O, a non-profit, grant-funded accelerator aiming to bring new solutions to global water challenges to the marketplace. It offers a virtual program on turning water challenges into business opportunities, including mentorship and access to customers and investors. It also organizes a boot camp. Imagine H$_2$O has supported over 550 startups in 30 countries. It has an annual ten-month program of about 10-12 startups in which no costs are involved. It takes no equity in its startups.

Ian Foraker, executive director of Cleantech Open, a large, non-profit accelerator of early-stage clean technology companies. Its mission is to find, fund, and foster entrepreneurs with ideas to solve our greatest environmental and energy challenges. It has a volunteer community that it relies on. Cleantech Open works with about 150 startups per year (across the U.S.). Awarded over $6 million; over 1,000 participating startups raised more than $1.1 billion. Cleantech Open is funded through sponsors, fees, and memberships. It offers mentoring, webinars, boot camps, events, a prize competition, and capital raising. It works on the basis of a participation fee. No office space is provided and it does not take equity in its startups.

Brian Hoffman, vice president of revenue and director of legal affairs at StartX, an educational, non-profit accelerator for Stanford University startup founders, from students to professors and alumni. StartX is industry and stage agnostic. Its programs are based on access to Stanford community, mentors, education, and resources. Offers one-to-one mentorship, drop-in office space, legal advice, and three ten-week sessions per year. It is backed by an uncapped StartX-Stanford Fund. StartX deployed over $90 million in 185 StartX companies. It boasts over 350 alumni companies, which have raised a total of over $1.9 billion. It offers a special medical program. StartX does not charge fees, and it does not take equity in its startups.

Ari Horie, founder and CEO at Women's Startup Lab, which aims to catalyze and empower women-run startups. Year-long program, of which two weeks is a residential program and six months is via remote coaching. It is highly selective and will take only a maximum of nine female founders. Its programs consist of workshops, coaching, network expansion, advising, leadership skills, assessments, and access to investors. Unique features are its high-impact engagement and interaction and its personal approach. It charges a $10,000 tuition fee.

Emily Kirsch, co-founder and CEO of Powerhouse, a for-profit but mission-driven incubator and accelerator for solar software startups. Powerhouse Accelerator offers a six-month program, two batches per year, eight startups in total. It has 14,000 square feet in co-working office space. Cold hard investments of $10,000. Startup investment up to $50,000; equity: 5%. One-to-one coaching, free office space, and access to investors and contacts in solar industries. Its workspace currently hosts 20 solar startups; nine solar organizations, and 80 solar entrepreneurs.

Cindy Klein-Marmer, associate director of the Butler Venture Accelerator Program of Babson College; branch in San Francisco. The program is for both students and alumni, and startups are aided in everything from ideation via business model, team recruiting, minimal viable product, and marketing to business launch and growth. Its resources include faculty advisors, outside mentors, work space, seed funding, legal advice, workshops, events, and peer groups. Offers a summer venture program and organizes a rocket pitch and a prize competition. Cross-campus collaboration. 365 entrepreneurs participated in 2015-2016.

Naomi Kokubo, co-founder and COO of Founders Space, a global, for-profit accelerator focused on educating and training seed startups as well as early-stage startups. It provides an online incubation program, innovation workshops, co-working space, startup pitch events, a two-week intensive startup accelerator program, a three-month online program as well as access to lawyers, marketers, VCs, serial entrepreneurs. Equity under 5%; startups may opt to pay a fee. Founders Space has a branch in Shanghai.

Duncan Logan, founder and CEO of RocketSpace, a large, co-working campus to help grow tech startups. It currently has 200 startups on its campus and has hosted more than 800 startups since 2011. RocketSpace offers 24/7 turnkey office solutions (private office, dedicated desk, drop-in desk); community education (workshops, speakers); access to VCs, mentors and advisors; and meeting and event spaces. 16 of its alumni companies are valued at over $1 billion. The average total of funds raised by startup members is $18 million; 1.5 startups secure funding per week. Special Industry Accelerator Program. It takes no equity in its startups.

T.M. Ravi, co-founder and managing director of The Hive, a small, co-creation studio and specialized fund focused on AI, context computing, autonomous agents, ambient intelligence, and blockchain. It targets startups in the enterprise, IoT, security, and financial services markets. Disruption driven by data. The Hive is involved in the intensive co-creation of new ventures and provides seed financing of $1.5 to $2 million. It takes in only four to five startups a year. Its equity policy is that if a company is started, The Hive also becomes a founder.

Prashant Shah, managing director of TiE LaunchPad, an accelerator dedicated to fostering entrepreneurship in the Bay Area with a focus on B2B startups, e.g. cloud apps, IT infrastructure, mobile, big data. Linked to TiE group, that has 13,000 members globally. The funding of startups is arranged through TiE Angels & TiE50 (awards program). Beyond idea stage; demo or prototype. Co-working space. Seasoned TiE entrepreneurs are startup mentors. TiE LaunchPad accepts eight companies per five-month batch. Funding $50,000; 4% equity.

Prem Talreja, vice president of marketing at The Fabric, an accelerator based on a collaboration model that works hands-on with startup entrepreneurs to help them refine their product, team, and business model and prepare them for series A funding. Seeds between $1 million to $1.5 million. Its focus is on cloud infrastructure technologies, and it has a Technology Innovation Lab in India. Only a few startups a year are accepted, for about six months. Network of mentors, investors, technologists, professionals. Equity proportional to investment.

Harm TenHoff, founder and CEO of BayLink, which combines a global medical incubator with a business accelerator. Its focus is on high-tech medical devices, life sciences, IT, and online retailing. Its incubator concentrates on product ideas and concepts, while its accelerator focuses on product introductions. It links Silicon Valley to Europe, and vice versa. BayLink offers one-on-one coaching and mentoring. Invests in kind, soft money. No cash investments. Its business model is based on consultancy fees and sometimes equity.

Marco ten Vaanholt, co-founder and managing partner at BootUP, a micro-ecosystem for startups to create better entrepreneurs and accelerate their companies. It works on the basis of four pillars. BootUP World is a Silicon Valley launch pad and global hub. BootUP Corporate Acceleration empowers corporate ventures. BootUP Capital accelerates and funds start-ups; post-seed and series A/B. BootUP Wings is a private club of startups, VCs, and seasoned Silicon Valley CEOs. It offers co-working space and currently has 55 startups under its wing. Takes equity, between 5-10% for early-stage and between 2-5% for later-stage companies.

Matt Walters, former managing director of Runway, a 30,000 square-foot co-working space and startup hub for new business incubation. It provides office space to about 80 startups and 200 entrepreneurs; educational events, lectures, and network meetings; access to VCs, legal advice, domain experts; a Zen area; and demo days. Valuations totaling over $600 million. Virtual EdTech accelerator; $25,000 future equity investment. Runway itself does not require equity.

Jun Wong, executive director of Hacker Dojo, "a community for hackers and startups" that supports everything from launching a software startup to building a robot. It hosts a mix of software developers and hardware engineers and offers them 24/7 co-working space, an events venue, maker space, seminars and workshops, code tutorials, parties, and a startup program. Hacker Dojo cherishes its community feeling and emphasizes participation. There is no selection process for members. Its business model is based on memberships, sponsoring, and donations. Hacker Dojo takes no equity in its startups.

Elizabeth Yin, partner at 500 Startups, a global venture capital seed fund and startup accelerator with over $250 million in assets. It has invested in over 1,800 startups from more than 60 countries and has had over 50 exits. Its accelerator programs emphasize internet marketing and customer acquisition, design and first-use experience, lean startup practices, and metrics. It has a four-month in-house program for four batches per year, with 40-50 startups per batch. 500 Startups provides 10,000 square feet in co-office space and organizes investor pitches, demo days, events, workshops, and presentations. $150,000 gross investment for 6% equity. $500K follow-on right.

1   Silicon Valley

The DNA of an Entrepreneurial Region

Introduction

For over half a century, Silicon Valley – the 60-mile strip in the Bay Area between San Francisco and San Jose – has been the world's premier high-tech hotspot for innovation and entrepreneurship. It houses more startups than any other region on the globe and has managed to perpetually renew itself. The Valley is a magnet for high-tech startup entrepreneurs who want to excel, and its business climate is based on a unique combination of talent, ideas, creativity, competitiveness, perseverance, and passion. It is an amazing innovative economy filled with ambitious entrepreneurs who are mission-driven and positively obsessed with the aim of disrupting existing markets and mainstream technologies. Silicon Valley is the headquarters of iconic high-tech companies such as Google, Apple, HP, Oracle, Cisco, Facebook, LinkedIn, Uber, Airbnb, WhatsApp, Twitter, Dropbox, Instagram, Salesforce, WMware, and many more: all innovation giants that have changed our lifestyles and our very way of thinking, working, and communicating, and which all began as small but eager startups. These high-tech companies have had an unparalleled social and economic impact and have inspired thousands of hungry startups to shoot for the moon as well. The fact that most startups fail to hit this objective is part of the prevailing Darwinian business logic in the Valley.

A few simple but telling statistics illustrate Silicon Valley's success in cultivating corporate and startup performance. It has been calculated that if the Bay Area, with Silicon Valley as its technological and economic nucleus, were a country, it would rank 19th in terms of GDP.[1] The Valley has the highest concentration of startups (between 14,000 and 19,000) in the world, and this has been the case for decades. It houses more U.S. and Global Fortune 500 companies than anywhere in the U.S. except for New York.[2] The region is home to the headquarters of practically all major social media companies as well as half of the top 100 U.S. private clean technology companies. Silicon Valley high-tech firms are worth over $3 trillion, hold more than one-third of U.S. corporate cash reserves, and earned over $100 billion in aggregated profits (in 2014). Five out of ten U.S. venture capital dollars are spent in Silicon Valley, mirroring the ample availability of VC (venture capital) funding there. It has launched more unicorns than any other place in the US. In

2014 alone, the Valley had 14 initial public offerings (IPOs: first sale of stock of a private company to the public), which was slightly less than 10% of the total number of U.S. IPOs in that year. The Valley's exit volume represents half of the value of startup exits within the top 20 global startup ecosystems and dominates these top rankings in terms of performance, funding, and talent.[3] Its focus on high tech is reflected by the large number of patents originating in the Valley: almost 16,000 in 2013 (13% of the U.S. total in that year). R&D is clearly vital for a region that makes its business out of innovation. Apple and Google, two leading Silicon Valley players, together spend over $12.5 billion on their R&D efforts. With world-class private and public universities such as Stanford and Berkeley in its midst, the Valley offers access to an abundant pool of talented graduates and high-quality fundamental and applied research. Moreover, the region is home to a large number of renowned corporate and non-corporate R&D labs.

All this happens in an area of some 1,800 square miles and a population of about three million people. Unlike in Europe, immigrant entrepreneurship flourishes in Silicon Valley: about half of all startups are founded by first-generation immigrants, particularly from India and China. Some immigrant entrepreneurs have become extremely successful and serve as important role models: they include Sergey Brin (Google), Andrew Grove (Intel), Vinod Khosla (Sun Microsystems), Jan Koum (WhatsApp), and Elon Musk (Tesla). Immigrant human capital is an indispensable part of the Silicon Valley saga. There is no Silicon Valley without its highly educated army of immigrant coders, software engineers, and technologists.

Europe and Silicon Valley

For many European countries, regions, and cities, Silicon Valley is the global paragon of innovation, startups, and high-tech entrepreneurship and a place they want to emulate. Cities such as London, Berlin, Paris, Amsterdam, Eindhoven, Barcelona, Madrid, Dublin, Milan, Tallinn, and Helsinki are quickly developing into profiled European startup innovation hubs.[4] Europe understands that it needs to invest in a dynamic startup economy and to boost entrepreneurship. The Netherlands, for instance, has concluded that it needs more ambitious entrepreneurship and has accelerated its agenda for innovative entrepreneurship and new ventures.[5] The European Union has declared that small and medium-sized enterprises (SMEs) must become more innovative if Europe is to strengthen its vulnerable post-crisis economy and to stimulate economic growth. In 2014, the EU launched its comprehensive *Horizon 2020* program to boost research and innovation. With nearly € 80 billion in funding made available, the program aims to enhance Europe's global competitiveness, drive sustainable economic growth, and create jobs.

Silicon Valley's innovation and startup architecture is a global benchmark. Every year this high-tech region is toured by busloads of European (and non-European) policymakers; politicians; entrepreneurs; venture capitalists and other investors; university representatives; and national, regional, and city authorities who want to learn from Silicon Valley – to taste its secret sauce, so to speak. They all want to see what makes the Valley tick, to understand the anatomy of this exceptional innovation area, and ultimately, of course, to explore what Europe needs to change in order to energize its level of competitive innovativeness and entrepreneurship. This is not an easy challenge. Major institutional and cultural obstacles need to be overcome, entrepreneurial attitudes must become stronger, governments must redefine their role, educational systems need to become more entrepreneurial, more venture capital must become available, and a more elaborate startup support infrastructure must be established.

In considering Silicon Valley as the startup and innovation mecca, Europe should understand that there are at least three constraints to adopting this model: the impact of path dependence, the role of culture, and the risk of an increase in social inequality. Let me briefly explain these issues.

Silicon Valley is not the intended outcome of an innovation and pro-entrepreneurship policy that was designed a priori. It was not created overnight, nor did it start as a technological *tabula rasa*. Rather, it is rooted in an innovation history that advanced through a series of technological paradigm shifts. The history of Silicon Valley, going back to the early 20th century, clearly embodies this primacy of path dependence (Scaruffi 2014; Sturgeon 2000). Its current high-tech dominance is embedded in a long chain of technological disruptions and innovation waves that spanned decades. It started with vacuum tube radio technology that later became a fruitful breeding ground for technologies such as microwave tubes, semiconductors, and integrated circuits (Lécuyer 2007).

Both World Wars, the Korean War, the Cold War, and the Space Race led to massive government spending on new defense technology from which Silicon Valley greatly benefited (Leslie 2000; Mazzucato 2014), spearheading the Valley's role as a center of innovation and technology. These developments in technology and their new applications paved the way for the more recent computer and software revolution, which quickly reached mass consumer markets – facilitated, of course, by the rapid expansion of the Internet. It spurred a seemingly never-ending stream of programs and applications – and, more recently, apps for smart phones and other mobile devices – that have penetrated the lives of billions of people. No domain, country, continent, or generation has remained untouched by this revolutionary acceleration of technological hardware and software applications, and Silicon Valley was and is a key disruptive game changer.

This path-dependence framework (Lebret 2007; Nelson & Winter 1982; Stangler 2013) implies that high-tech innovation regions such as Silicon Valley cannot be copied for the simple reason that its history cannot be replicated. It also entails that creating European innovation hubs will only work when based on a proved innovation infrastructure and network of high-tech companies, or, as I argue in the next chapter, an advanced ecosystem. Excellence in innovation is not something that can be attained from thin air; it takes a technological environment and innovation setting that have some degree of sophistication and maturity. Regions and cities that dream of having their own Silicon Valley but lack a supportive ecosystem will not see their dreams become reality.

The second constraint is the role of culture. The Silicon Valley innovation and startup model is rooted in a culture that cherishes an entrepreneurial mindset and big ideas but also openness, sharing, drive, achievement, and commitment. The model is based on a culture that prizes risk-taking and accepts failing; one that calls for pro-active networking and fearless self-presentation; one that favors thinking big, encourages disruption, promotes diversity, and takes persistence and hard work for granted. It is the combination of these cultural characteristics that is at the core of the Silicon Valley model. The European willingness to learn from Silicon Valley will only pay off if we take these cultural prerequisites seriously. Changing the prevalent culture in European countries with respect to an innovation mindset, entrepreneurship, and work attitudes takes time, in some cases even generations. Cultural change cannot be decreed from above but rather is a long-term process in which education plays a key role.

Fortunately, European leaders realize that Europe needs to address its entrepreneurial deficit and revolutionize its culture of entrepreneurship. In the revealing words of the European Commission: "there is (...) a widespread culture that does not recognize or reward entrepreneurial endeavors enough and does not celebrate successful entrepreneurs, as role models who create jobs and income. To make entrepreneurship the growth engine of our economy Europe needs a thorough, far-reaching cultural change."[6] The European Startup Manifesto (2013) underlines this need for Europe to effect a change in culture: "To create more businesses and more startups requires more than a change in policy. It requires a change in mentality."

The third issue – the risk of an increase in social inequality – is of a different nature and relates to the underlying social model of Silicon Valley, a model that embraces the ideal of meritocracy and a winner-takes-all mentality. Though the Valley is a prosperous region with the highest per-capita incomes in the U.S., it is also home to blatant social inequality: its wealth is very unevenly divided over the various population groups. African-Americans and Hispanics in particular are overrepresented among the less privileged segments. Income gaps are widening. The high-tech economy may be booming but so are housing prices and the cost of living, squeezing the lower and middle class out of the Valley and out of San Francisco. Wealth polarization is painful. This is also part of the Silicon Valley story, and Europe needs to agree on what deviations from the European social model it is willing to accept and where it should draw the line between meritocracy and social equality, between the individual pursuit of happiness and the collective goal of solidarity, between exclusion and cohesion. From an anthropological point of view, the Silicon Valley model is based on an almost 'hubristic' paradigm and an overconfident conception of man, whereas incrementalism and a step-by-step approach is more characteristic of the European psyche.

These three basic constraints lead to the conclusion that the Silicon Valley innovation and startup model cannot simply be copied by European policymakers and stakeholders. Replication will not work because preconditions cannot be met (path dependence, culture) or necessitate a social debate (inequality). But this conclusion, it must be stressed, is the *beginning* of the policy discussion and not the end. Europe needs to commit itself to building a competitive startup economy, but in doing so it must find and develop its own model – a model that fits its core values, its cultural challenges, and the history of its technology.

Accelerators: Pillars of Silicon Valley's startup support infrastructure

Having said all this, there is much that European policymakers, innovation stakeholders, and startup founders can learn from Silicon Valley. One of the cornerstones of the Valley's advanced ecosystem is the role played by for-profit and non-profit accelerators that help startups in commercializing their business ideas. There is a vast infrastructure of accelerators in Silicon

Valley that assists startup founders in developing their product (or service), in strengthening their team, in working towards a MVP (minimum viable product), in designing a business and marketing plan, in attracting funding and investors, in coaching and mentoring the startup team, in bringing the product to the market, and in getting first customers and achieving traction. This refined accelerator support structure is a key feature of the Silicon Valley innovation and startup model (Bay Area Council Economic Institute 2016).[7] The approaches and business models of accelerators differ considerably (CBIA 2016). Some accelerators are large, some are small; some have specific target groups, others welcome a diverse array of entrepreneurs; some focus on specific technologies, others are more general; some accelerators take equity, others do not. Some offer office space, others work online. But they all share the same ambition to help startups to succeed.

These 'schools of startup entrepreneurship' flourish and are an intrinsic part of the way Silicon Valley innovates and launches new startups.[8] Because they service new ventures with an integral offer of resources, coaching, and networks, they empower startup teams to make their business viable. Serious startups are thus keen to be admitted to an acclaimed accelerator. It enhances their market chances and funding opportunities. "A stepping-stone towards further financing", according to Højer Nicolaj Nielsen (2017: 100), well-known Danish serial entrepreneur and business angel. But competition is tough, as demand does not match supply by any measure. It is extremely difficult to get into the top accelerators. Accelerators' rates of rejection are considerable; the entry bar is set high.

The economic impact of accelerators is substantial. CBIA (2016) has calculated that portfolio companies from accelerators (and incubators) in California have raised $16.9 billion in cumulative funding since 2004. The average accelerator injects over $400,000 annually in its local economy. Two-thirds of accelerators invest directly in the startups they admit into their programs. Accelerators, CBIA concludes, "have become a key ingredient to supporting new generations of startups, whether they are corporate, non-profit, academic, or private." (2016: 7). Their graduates "have harnessed those resources for expansion in the U.S. and the world, and have invested in new jobs, facilities, and equipment, while spending extends to every corner of the world."[9] Brad Feld, co-founder of Techstars, one of the earliest U.S. accelerators, even speaks of an 'accelerator movement' that has fundamentally changed the way companies are created.[10]

I believe that in its ambition to upgrade its startup infrastructure, Europe can greatly benefit from having a closer look at how Silicon Valley has developed its accelerator support system. This is precisely the goal of this study: to share the main findings, conclusions, and recommendations of the research I conducted among a significant sample of Silicon Valley accelerators with European policymakers, scholars, students, entrepreneurs, and startup founders. I believe that the way these accelerators operate can serve as examples for Europe in its development of a more professional startup support system.

In this descriptive study, I examine the way Silicon Valley accelerators operate in priming startups for the marketplace. Based on a series of interviews with accelerators in the Valley, I outline the different underlying business philosophies of accelerators and the target startups they focus on. I also describe the accelerators' unique selling points (USPs) as well as the rigorous way they select the startups that will enter their program. Furthermore, I report on the content and intensity of the accelerator programs with respect to product development, team building, coaching, mentoring, networking, funding, and support facilities. What is crucial, of course, is the access of accelerators to angel investors, VCs, and investor funds. I analyze the business models that accelerators are based on and their startup funding options (e.g., equity). Likewise, I describe the networks that accelerators are involved in, the way they cooperate with external partners, the challenges they see, and future plans they may have (including expanding their business to Europe). Finally, I examine the perceived success of accelerators. How effective accelerators are in growing and scaling startups is a topic that has been much debated in the literature and in the public discourse. Is there a strong correlation – or even a causal relationship – between accelerator participation and startup success? Settling this issue is beyond the scope of this study, but in my interviews I invited the chief executives of accelerators to reflect on these matters.

Accelerators mentor and facilitate startups in the process of making their new product or service market-ready. Let's take a look at how some accelerators market themselves, often peppered with a dose of positive Californian bravado. RocketSpace prides itself on its alumni such as Dropbox, Spotify, and Uber, stating that: "We help bring the future to the market. Our campus is a tech startup's paradise. We've designed the perfect ecosystem that fosters networking, community, and innovation specifically to help startups to thrive." 500 Startups, which has funded successful startups such as Twilio, Credit Karma, MakeBot, Wildfire, and Viki, brands itself as "a startup MBA on steroids". Tandem's mission is to back "the next generation of disruptive entrepreneurs", and HAX defines itself as "the world's first and largest hardware accelerator". Runway's passion is to be "the workplace for innovators", and The Hive's vision is to "change the world with artificial intelligence".

Corporate accelerator Samsung NEXT's drive is to partner with (startup) entrepreneurs "wherever they are and empower them with what they need to go farther, faster." Plug and Play, an investor in numerous startups including PayPal, SoundHound, and LendingClub, claims to be "the world's biggest startup accelerator (...) which produces unbelievable success stories every day". Modesty and unpretentiousness are not concepts that dominate the Silicon Valley dictionary of entrepreneurship, to put it mildly. Instead, "Think Big, Aim High" is the leading mantra, mirroring the ambition, passion, and spirit of entrepreneurship that are embedded in the Valley.

Accelerators: their role, research, and results

Empirical studies on the role of accelerators in launching startups are very scarce (Dempwolf et al. 2014). This lack of systematic research can be attributed to the simple fact that accelerators are a relatively new phenomenon. Pioneering accelerators such as Y Combinator (Mountain View, California), Techstars (Boulder, Colorado), and Seedcamp (London) were created only ten years ago, and the rapid growth of accelerators in Silicon Valley and elsewhere has only taken place in the last five years. The implication of this short history is that there is only limited comparable data available on the effectiveness of accelerators (GALI 2016; Cohen & Hochberg 2014; Miller & Bound 2011). For-profit accelerators, moreover, are not obliged to publicize details about their startup growth programs.

There is some conceptual confusion, too. This begins with the definition of what an accelerator is. One of the issues here is the validity of the distinction between an incubator and an accelerator. There is an ongoing debate in the academic and popular literature on the relevance of this distinction, and definitions differ considerably (CBIA 2016; Deering 2014; Nielsen 2017; Van Weele 2016). The first-generation incubators – which emerged in Europe in the 1980s and in Silicon Valley in the late 1950s – primarily offered co-working office space and were based on a real estate business model. They supplied new ventures with economy-of-scale advantages. Examples are science parks and shared office buildings. The second-generation incubators, which emerged in the early 1990s, added an in-house support service structure including training and coaching as well as some funding. The third-generation incubators came onto the scene in the late 1990s, offering a more extended portfolio that provided access to networks and external resources such as venture capital (Van Weele 2016; Grimaldi & Grandi 2005, 2012; Bruneel et al. 2012; Mian et al. 2016, Pauwels et al. 2016).

Accelerators, which were launched in the last five to ten years, might be seen as fourth-generation incubators or, alternatively, as startup growth facilities of their own, as they differ from typical mainstream incubators. An accelerator can be defined as a miniature or micro-ecosystem that helps startups to rapidly grow their business, offering a broad scope of support and facilities such as coaching, mentoring, and training; fine-tuning product-market fit; providing access to investors, networks, and clients; and creating a learning community of practice and peers.

Inspired by recent contributions by CBIA (2016), Nielsen (2017), Cohen & Hochberg (2014), Miller & Bound (2011), and Dempwolf et al. (2014), I identify a number of features that differentiate accelerators from incubators. These include the admissions process, duration, funding, program intensity, teams, culture, and cohorts.[11] Accelerators apply highly competitive and restrictive selection procedures: only the most promising startups are admitted. The screening process is scrupulous, and only a small percentage of startups make the cut. By contrast, incubators have open admissions policies and are solely restricted by limited office space. The duration of accelerator programs is deliberately short and in most cases lasts up to three months. Accelerated startup business cycles may speed up growth or may hasten failure. Graduation from an incubator, however, may take up to five years and occurs within a generally protective environment, often framed as a 'safe haven' for nurturing new businesses (Bergek & Norrman 2014). Funding also differs. Privately owned accelerators provide admitted startups with some funding in return for equity or convertible notes, as they primarily aim to develop a profitable portfolio of seed-stage investments. By contrast, many incubators are publicly owned and not based on a business model that centers on financial participation in new ventures. Accelerators seek startup growth and scale that allows for a profitable exit (i.e., going public through an IPO or getting acquired by another firm), while the rent-seeking business model of incubators is by definition based on delayed exits and prolonged stays. Coaching, training, mentoring, and networking are provided by accelerators on a much more extensive and intensive basis than incubators do, something economist Ian Hathaway (2016a) describes as 'immersive education'. Offering 'smart capital' by seasoned entrepreneurs is a defining characteristic of professional accelerators. The focus on startup teams rather than on individual entrepreneurs is a further trait of accelerators, while incubators do not have distinct entry policies in this respect. Accelerators, furthermore, are usually very outspoken in their preference for startup founder teams, as they believe complementary skill sets are needed that as a rule cannot be embodied in one person. According to the logic of accelerators, growing a startup is a team effort and is simply too much for one individual. Accelerators endeavor to create a vibrant, high-pressure environment and an entrepreneurial pro-innovation culture that reinforces competition, performance, and rapid growth. This is much less the case for incubators. A final basic difference between accelerators and incubators is that startup teams in larger accelerators enter and graduate in groups, also known as batches or cohorts. This fosters bonds between startups, enables peer group support, and cultivates a shared identity between founders in the same cohort. The admissions procedure in incubators, as mentioned, is on a continuous basis, dependent on available office space.

It should be noted that these seven features I use to distinguish accelerators from incubators result in Weberian ideal-type representations of the two startup growth facilitators. In reality, as we will see, the distinction between incubators and accelerators is less clear-cut and more diffuse, as these defining features are not necessarily fully represented in concrete examples. There is clearly a gray area (CBIA 2016). Consequently, the taxonomy is instrumental rather than conceptual; it mainly points to operational differences.[12] Deering (2014: 13) uses a simple but clarifying analogy to explain these differences: "Incubators can be thought of as startup gyms – equipped with the necessary resources, environment, and guidance to grow your startup – while accelerators can be thought of as startup boot camps – just as equipped as incubators, but involving a more defined mission, application process, methodology for progress, and stakeholders. All in all, accelerators tend to focus more deliberately on achieving certain success criteria for a startup."

Van Weele (2016) recently published an important study on the role of accelerators (though he uses the term incubators) in varying national contexts. I particularly like the three theoretical frameworks he offers to explore the mechanisms and practices of the startup incubation and growth process. The first framework is the Resource Based View (RBV), which identifies the main tangible and intangible resources that accelerators provide to startups in order to increase their competitive advantage: office space, funding, knowledge, and networks. Startups struggle to accumulate resources that are necessary for product market launch, and accelerators help them to overcome this basic deficit. The second framework consists of theories on Organizational Learning (OL), which define entrepreneurship as a learning process in which startup teams learn by doing. In this perspective, accelerators aim to boost the teams' learning curve. The third theoretical framework states that starting entrepreneurs learn through active participation in Communities of Practice (CoP). Accelerators provide such a community-learning environment by sharing expertise, practices, and challenges and by creating an internal culture that shapes startup identity and generates entrepreneurship, passion, energy, and competition.

These three theoretical frames of reference are important because they focus on specific support processes and attributes that add to accelerators' potency in bringing startups to the marketplace. These accelerating mechanisms, according to Van Weele, may directly or indirectly support startup performance. Networking is a powerful aspect of the accelerating process. The accelerators' networks "contribute to startup performance by enabling startups to access missing resources, to efficiently acquire market, business, and technological knowledge, to gain legitimacy and to overcome challenges in the entrepreneurial ecosystem" (Van Weele 2016: 250). Accelerators, furthermore, may facilitate 'higher learning': a process in which startup teams come to question the assumptions underlying their new business, which may lead them to experiment with their product or even to radically change their business model.

Pauwels et al. (2016) investigated accelerators across Europe and came up with three basic types: the ecosystem builder, the deal-flow maker, and the welfare stimulator. The ecosystem builder is an accelerator that is often created by corporates as a matchmaking device linking startups with customers and stakeholders, which in turn creates an entrepreneurial ecosystem around the corporate company. The deal-flow maker typifies an accelerator that is funded by VCs, angels, and investment funds with the primary goal of selecting promising startups for investment purposes. The welfare stimulator is commonly an accelerator backed by government stakeholders in order to promote startup communities and economic growth centered on certain technological themes and domains.

Though research on accelerator effectiveness is scarce, there is a handful of research studies that we can consult. One study by Hallen et al. (2014) showed that accelerator-backed new ventures were faster at raising venture capital and at gaining customer traction than similar non-accelerator ventures. Winston-Smith & Hannigan (2015) found that accelerator graduate startups were more likely to raise next-round financing sooner than non-graduates and had a higher chance of exiting by acquisition or by quitting.[13] A 2016 study by the Global Accelerator Learning Initiative also indicated that accelerator startup graduates managed to raise larger new investments. Fehder & Hochberg (2015) concluded that accelerators have a positive impact on regional ecosystems, particularly by having more seed and early-stage entrepreneurial financing activity. But, again, it has to be emphasized that these studies are early accounts of accelerators' effectiveness. Performance metrics based on comparable longitudinal data are rare. We need much more empirical data and case studies on how accelerators are doing in terms of effectively growing and scaling startups, and not only in Silicon Valley. Having such metrics would greatly enhance our understanding of how accelerators operate and what determines its achievements.

Methodology

This study is part of a broader research program aimed at understanding and explaining why Silicon Valley has succeeded in becoming the global center for innovative startups and cutting-edge entrepreneurship. This larger research program is based on a variety of data collection methods, using different primary and secondary sources. Based on these insights, I come up with recommendations for improving Europe's policy towards startups. The ecosystem concept is a key notion in the way I frame the Silicon Valley success story. A reconstruction of the Silicon Valley ecosystem shows how this region's economic and technological track record is rooted in a set of advanced institutional and cultural factors that fuel innovation and new ventures. It is an ecosystem that manages to renew itself continuously and that spurs talented startups. My book *Silicon Valley: Planet Startup* (2016), co-authored by Arne Maas, attempts to portray this remarkably well-advanced ecosystem and to demonstrate how it lays the foundation for a thriving startup community.

Over the past years, I took various research trips to the Valley to interview numerous startup founders and CEOs in the area; consulted local domain experts, entrepreneurs, and business representatives; had conversations with colleagues from the Bay Area universities; spoke with economic think tanks and chambers of commerce; talked with policymakers and politicians; organized group interviews with students; studied the history of Silicon Valley; and reviewed the scholarly and popular literature on the Valley's success and impact.[14] I furthermore interviewed VCs and angels, attended angel funding pitch rounds, went to startup events and network meet-ups, drank numerous *lattes* in startup cafes in SoMa– the neighborhood in San Francisco that is home to many startups– and, of course, visited the Valley's iconic high-tech corporates.

As explained above, accelerators are pillars of Silicon Valley's highly developed ecosystem. Some of them have launched mega-successful startups. On an aggregate level, they receive thousands of applications a year. Because accelerators need to be both profiled and visible to startups and funders, most of them are fairly well known. This makes it relatively easy for a study such as this one to identify accelerators, even if their numbers are rapidly growing (CBIA 2016). The first methodological step was to reduce the long list of accelerators to a meaningful short list of about twenty to twenty-five companies where an in-person interview could be arranged. A transparent set of criteria was used to facilitate the selection procedure. The sample I ended up with is a fair representation of the following six accelerator features: profit vs. not-for-profit, general vs. specific focus, taking equity vs. not-taking equity, large vs. small accelerators, offering workspace vs. virtual program, short vs. longer programs. I allowed myself some flex- ibility in applying these criteria, also in view of the overlapping gray area between accelerators and incubators. And finally, the accelerators in my study needed to be in business for at least two to three years.[15]

With this set and with the help of some well-known key persons in my Silicon Valley network (see Acknowledgements), accelerators were selected and approached by email for a personal interview. Most of the accelerators accepted the interview invitation, some of them did not respond, and one declined because of lack of time. All the accelerators that were directly linked to me via email by my key contact people agreed to be interviewed, illustrating the strength of networks in the Valley. This non-probability sampling procedure worked well: a total of twenty-three accelerators could be interviewed (see Appendix 1). Two accelerators were interviewed in the autumn of 2015, twenty accelerators in the summer of 2016, and one in the autumn of 2016. The two accelerator interviews held in 2015 were part of my fieldwork for the previous book project but fit well into this research study and were therefore included. Twenty-one interviews were conducted face-to-face, and two interviews were conducted via Skype. Eight of the twenty-three selected accelerators are based in San Francisco, fourteen in Silicon Valley, and one in nearby Oakland. All the interviewees are accelera- tor founders and/or chief executives. Three of the accelerators in my sample rank in the top nine best performing accelerators in the United States: 500 Startups, the Alchemist Accelerator, and StartX.[16] Four of the accelerators are in the top ten global accelerators for overseas startups: Founders Space, Plug and Play, 500 Startups, and HAX.[17]

The questionnaire I used is thematically structured and clustered around a number of subjects relating to the way accelerators operate and to the conceptual model outlined in the next chapter. The main topics covered are: accelerator philosophy, perceived unique selling points, startup intake and selection procedure, technology focus and startup target group, funding and business model, accelerator program characteristics, perceived accelerator challenges, cooperation partners, success attribution, and future plans (see Appendix 2). Although the questionnaire is quite lengthy, all the interviews were without exception animated, open, informative, and very pleasant. Interviewees were genuinely interested in the topics of the interview, and the conversations were energetic and lively. The length of the interview varied between 60 and 90 minutes.[18] With the exception of the two Skype interviews, I conducted all the interviews at the accelerator itself, in most cases preceded or followed by an on-site guided workspace tour.[19] This provided *couleur locale* and a good impression of the accelerator in action. It also offered an opportunity for me to talk to startup teams that were taking part in the accelerator program.

With the interviewees' permission, the interviews were recorded digitally.[20] Transcripts were made by Flatworld Solutions, a specialized transcription service in Bangalore, India.[21] Three random quality checks per interview were done by the research team, and no irregularities were observed. All the interviews were analyzed by Atlas.ti, a professional software program for qualitative data. Interviewees gave their consent for me to publish quotes from the interviews.[22] Two of my respondents changed jobs in the period between the interview and the finalization of the manuscript. Doug Davenport, founder and CEO of Prospect SV, is now on its Board of Directors. Matt Walters, the managing director of Runway, is now general partner at Mission VC. TiE LaunchPad's three-year lifecycle was concluded at the end of 2016 and has since continued as TiE Angels. Additional secondary data collection on accelerators' performance and portfolio was closed on March 31, 2017; developments after this date could not been included.

I decided to write this study in a way that allows the accelerator founders and CEOs to tell their own story of how they help startups to accelerate growth and scalability, their accelerator philosophy, their accelerator programs, their showcases, the challenges they encounter, and their ambitions for the future. I feel that this writing method adds to the readability of the study and helps me to communicate my main findings to my European target group in a more convincing way.

Overview

This book is structured as follows. In chapter 2, an attempt is made to explain why Silicon Valley is such a globally successful region in terms of innovation and entrepreneurship. The conceptual model that will be introduced stresses the particular way in which cultural and institutional factors interact in this region. The model emphasizes that pro-innovation cultural factors such as thinking big, the tolerance of failure, the preference for openness and sharing, the eagerness to compete and to excel, and an entrepreneurial mindset constitute an extraordinary fertile breeding ground for a thriving startup community. Institutional factors such as access to talent, access to funding, a pro-active government, and an effective new venture support system are equally relevant in understanding Silicon Valley's high-tech startup success story. Accelerators, I will argue, are in essence intentional micro representations of this unique combination of cultural and structural factors. They are a focal element of the Valley's startup support infrastructure.

The chapters that follow examine the views of the accelerators' chief executives on their role in this infrastructure and their opinions on the various topics covered by this study: accelerators' selection procedure, business model and funding; the features of accelerators' programs; startup coaching and team mentorship; success and fail factors; and accelerators' challenges and future plans. Chapter 3 describes some of the chief differences between the accelerators with respect to their philosophy of supporting and growing startups, whether they specialize in certain technology sectors or have a more general scope, and how they collaborate with external partners. The chapter also explores the various accelerator business models. What is the underlying revenue matrix of profit and not-for-profit accelerators, and what are the different funding options (e.g., equity requirements) they offer to startups? Chapter 4 reports on how accelerators organize the selection and intake process for startups to enter their programs. How restrictive are accelerators, what are the main selection criteria, and what is their rejection rate? What qualities do they prioritize among startup teams?

The accelerator startup programs themselves are analyzed in some detail in chapter 5. I look at the nature, frequency, intensity, and duration of the various programs. The chapter shows that accelerators differ markedly in this respect, as they look for distinct market niches, competitive advantages, and market or mission-driven technology segments. Chapter 6 outlines the chief executives' beliefs about why some accelerator startups succeed while others fail. Is there a basic pattern, or do causes differ substantially? What are the accelerated startups they are most proud of and why? And what do executives perceive as the most pressing challenges their accelerator faces, and what are their plans for the future? Do they plan to pivot their own strategy? Chapter 7, finally, puts the main findings into perspective and formulates a set of core conclusions and policy recommendations. What lessons can Europe draw? What roles can profit and non-profit accelerators play in implementing an inspiring and challenging new European startup agenda? To conclude the book, I offer a practical decision tool that will help European stakeholders and entrepreneurs in making the basic choices of setting up accelerators.

2 Innovation and Startups in Silicon Valley

An Ecosystem Approach

Modeling the Valley's ecosystem[23]

In order to understand and explain Silicon Valley's long-standing performance as a global engine of innovation, entrepreneurship, and startups, I developed a model that stresses the interrelatedness of cultural and institutional factors at the micro, meso, and macro level of this high-tech region (Ester & Maas 2016: 29-41). I define Silicon Valley as a well-integrated and balanced ecosystem in which all constituting elements are lined up to promote and sustain leading-edge innovation and pioneering entrepreneurship. It is an almost organic and prototypical system that generates an enduring and resilient habitat for innovation and startups to thrive (Munroe 2009). The Valley is an environment that is built on the right cultural mindset and resource availability, which encourages and strengthens innovation and the founding of new ventures. Above all, it is an environment that stimulates a pro-innovation and entrepreneurial way of thinking that helps the creation of new businesses through a well-oiled network providing access to talent, knowledge, funding, mentoring, and legal counseling, and to accelerators. In the words of John-Seeley-Brown, the former chief scientist of Xerox, Silicon Valley is an ecosystem in which the different parts reinforce one another to create a "perpetual innovation machine".[24] It is an ecosystem that favors competition, disruptive thinking, and excellence and that supports startup teams to work on their dreams and to market their new business ideas. It is a habitat that fuels the fast growth of existing companies and has led to a booming startup economy that many other regions in the world are eager to learn from.

The ecosystem approach has proven to be a useful tool in analyzing innovation regions such as Silicon Valley (Bay Area Council Economic Institute 2012; Kenny 2000; Barami & Evans 1995; Brown & Duguid 2000; Moon Lee et al. 2000; for Europe: European Commission 2014; Startup Genome 2012, 2017; Telefónica 2013). It provides an integral and systematic insight into the characteristics that matter for regions to become and remain innovative and entrepreneurial, taking both cultural and institutional parameters into consideration (Porter 1990, 1998). The ecosystem approach, moreover, is by nature multidisciplinary and is an instrumental aid for policymakers to assess national or regional innovation strength, entrepreneurial efficacy, and startup potency.[25] By identifying the cultural and institutional preconditions that must be present for nations, regions, and cities to be innovative, competitive, and attractive for startups, the approach enables the benchmarking of startups and innovation areas at an international level. The figure below pictures the Silicon Valley Innovation and Startup Model, which distinguishes three interacting levels of this innovation and startup ecosystem interacting levels of this innovation and startup ecosystem.[26]

Figure 2.1.   The Silicon Valley Innovation and Startup Model

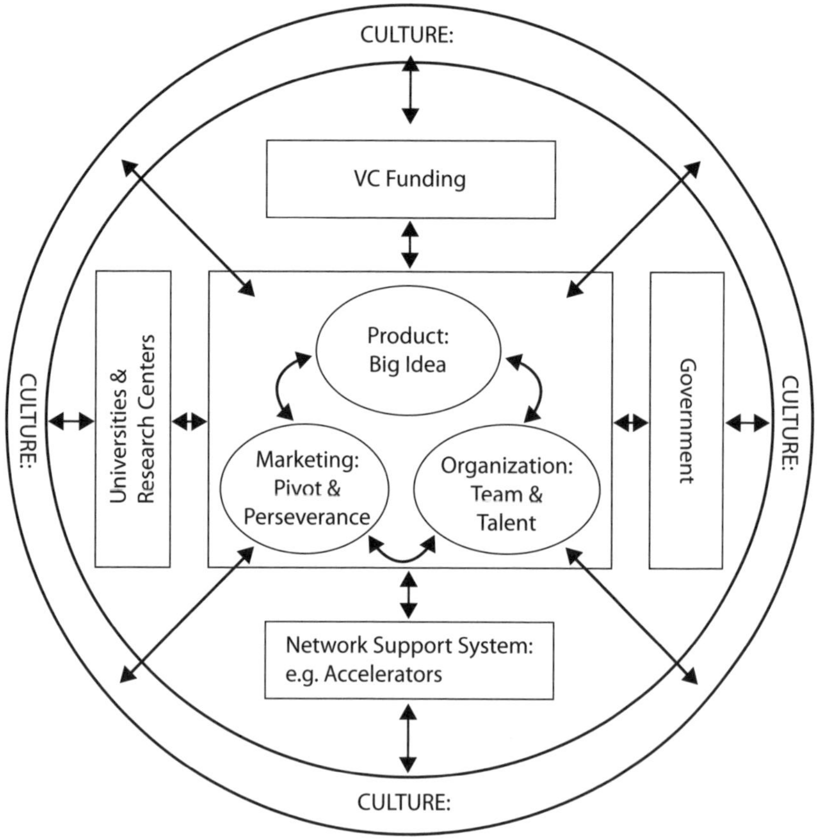

Source: Ester & Maas (2016: 41)

The *micro level* (center block, inner ring) specifies three main factors that relate to how expected startup success is framed in the Valley: the startup must be based on a Big Idea that will really shake and change the market (product), the new venture must be headed by a strong team that succeeds in hiring the best and most gifted talents available (team & talent), and the founders need to be capable of timely pivoting their original startup business strategy when circumstances rapidly change (pivot & perseverance).

The *meso level* (outer blocks, inner ring) identifies four institutions that have been decisive in building up Silicon Valley's startup ecosystem: access to ample VC new business funding; access to high-caliber universities and research centers that excel in innovation, work closely with industry, and actively promote new ventures; a government that invests in innovation and believes in a startup economy and is a launching customer of innovative products and a setter of market rules; and the presence of a strong network system of startup support agencies such as accelerators, legal counselors, and mentors.

The *macro level* (outer ring) points to the typical Silicon Valley culture that applauds entrepreneurship and shares innovation, favors the passionate pursuit of big dreams, emphasizes openness and learning, is risk prone and tolerates failure, and has the right startup frame of mind.[27] It is a culture that impacts the other two levels as well.

The figure above outlines the three levels, the corresponding factors, as well as their interrelationships that in my view define the main cultural and institutional ingredients of how Silicon Valley became the global engine of innovative startups.

As indicated in the model, accelerators (lower center block, inner ring) are part of Silicon Valley's advanced network support system. They help startups in their process of developing and pivoting their product and bringing it to market, they refine their business model and marketing strategy, they train founding teams and their skill sets, they offer access to funding, they assist them in getting their first customers and sales, and they provide a zesty accelerator startup culture. The model underlines the major role that accelerators play in Silicon Valley in launching startups.

Once again, it must be emphasized that it has taken Silicon Valley many decades to develop this well-functioning system and that its success is based on the intelligent combination of all of the ecosystem's constitutive features. The sum of the Silicon Valley ecosystem is more than its parts. This axiom illustrates again that selective cherry picking will not work in an attempt to replicate Silicon Valley's success elsewhere in the world. It is, simply said, all or nothing.

The model in more detail

The business anatomy of Silicon Valley is dominated by a unique combination of a pro-innovation and pro-startup culture and the prevalence of institutions that help new ventures to excel. In this chapter, I take a closer look at these cultural and institutional factors by describing and examining the different micro, meso, and macro levels of the Silicon Valley innovation and startup model. This context information will help to clarify the specific role and position of accelerators in the Silicon Valley ecosystem. The chapter attempts to give a broad overview of the way the Silicon Valley ecosystem functions, which will facilitate our understanding of how accelerators contribute to this self-reinforcing system. I begin with the micro level by exploring the way that innovation works in Silicon Valley, the necessary startup alignment of upstream and downstream innovation, the emphasis on disruptive innovation, the importance of strong startup teams, and the need for timely product pivoting by startups.

The micro level: Product, people, and pivot

Product: "Think big"
"Think big" is at the top of Silicon Valley's canon of innovation. Its mainstream business model is all about scale, the ambition to reach large markets, and the desire to have a social impact. Although "small is beautiful" is a philosophy and movement with Californian roots, it is definitely not how the Valley sees innovation and entrepreneurship. The very essence of high tech is that it is not limited by geographical boundaries such as regional or national home markets. As Marc Andreessen, one of the Valley's most reputable VCs, once said: "software is eating the world".[28] The Silicon Valley business model is based on scalability, preferably at the global level. The enormous success of high-tech companies such as Apple, Google, LinkedIn, Twitter, WhatsApp, Instagram, etc. can be attributed to the fact that their products service markets in virtually all corners of the world. Their market is not the Valley, not California, not even the U.S. – their market is the world. They are global brands with global customers, and with global impact. Scalability is what startups are evaluated on by investors; it is their prime funding criterion. "It's all about scale for VCs," according to Silicon Valley investor Marc Philips (2013: 15). And startups for their part know that they are being assessed in terms of their product scalability. There is not much sense for startups being in Silicon Valley with a product that is hardly scalable (or duplicable) and that is restricted

to quantitatively limited markets. Their prospects for funding are meager, if not non-existent.

Related to scale is the need for fast startup growth: entrepreneurs need to launch a scalable product that will quickly sell to sizeable volumes of customers. VCs constantly search for early-stage startups that develop products that combine scalability and fast growth. Silicon Valley unicorns such as Airbnb, Palantir, Dropbox, Uber, Pinterest, and WhatsApp all share these two fundamental success qualities: they reach substantial global customer segments and they have fast growth records. Accelerators, as I will conclude, are particularly keen on launching startups with scalability and growth potential. It is a vital part of their startup recruitment procedure and training program. It opens access to investors in their continuous search for the Next Big Thing, i.e. innovations beyond Google, Apple, or Facebook that will revolutionize the technological landscape and herald a new paradigm shift as well as mass markets, of course.

Scale and growth are key, but so is the innovation mission: the need to have a social impact and to offer practical solutions to pressing social issues. The Silicon Valley vocabulary overflows with phrases that grasp this fundamental ambition of startups to develop technologies "that will change the world" – not a very humble ambition but definitely one that dominates the Silicon Valley startup jargon. It is also sometimes called the "big hairy audacious goal". Apple founder Steve Jobs probably set the stage for this with his legendary statement: "we're here to put a dent in the universe". In pitching their product, Silicon Valley startups typically incorporate this mission-driven mantra of making the world a better place, though sometimes to the point of near meaninglessness. They know they should not settle for less and that the bar is raised high.[29]

The call to "think big" is a chronic part of the Silicon Valley narrative, indicated by its emphasis on scale, growth, and impact. But there is another dimension to this narrative: "think disruptive". The history of Silicon Valley is a history of disruptive technological breakthroughs, of Schumpeterian creative destruction.[30] These are technological changes that have radically transformed markets and playing fields, disruptive innovations that have redefined ruling technologies, outperformed existing markets, and attracted new consumer segments (Christensen 1997; Moore 2014). These innovations have shaken up the status quo, allowing new business models to emerge that drastically altered prevailing market relations. Uber shook up the taxi market, Airbnb upset the hotel market, Skype and WhatsApp disrupted the phone market, Amazon disturbed the book market, eBay changed the shopping market, and Spotify was a bomb under the CD market. And some decades earlier, the PC became a major competitor for expensive mainframe computers and totally broke up the computer hardware market and later also the software market. Disruptive innovation is in Silicon Valley's veins. It reshapes markets, introduces new competitors, and creates a significant impact. The Valley has embraced the idea of disruptive innovation to a nearly messianic degree, supported by its series of conferences, events, and meetings that celebrate disruptive innovation and its many merits.[31] Various accelerators, as we will see, explicitly aim for disruptive innovation.

Silicon Valley lives off innovation. Bringing to market new technologies, new products, and new software and hardware is the quintessence of its existence. "Think innovation" is the backbone of the Valley.[32] Entrepreneurial innovativeness and innovative entrepreneurship are bearers of the Silicon Valley narrative. Startups play a crucial role in this narrative, as they are pioneers in the innovation trajectory and in the commercialization of new technologies, products, and services. They are frontrunners, and as the new generation of business innovators, they challenge existing high-tech companies and dominant market positions. As new ventures, they are essential links in the chain of disruptive innovations.

People: Team and talent

Founding a startup is no small thing. Team, talent, and persistent optimism are absolutely indispensable in building a strong startup. It takes a lot to start a new business. Startup entrepreneurs must turn their business idea into a viable and competitive product, do the market math, secure funding, attract customers, develop a marketing strategy, structure the organization, hire and coach talent, and take timely decisions to pivot. Apart from serial entrepreneurs, startup founders tend to lack an entrepreneurial skill set based on prior business experience, but somehow they must survive in a mega-competitive environment of thousands of new ventures that all aim high, all want to make a difference, and all want a piece of the market pie. Founders need to cope with such daily hurdles as cash flow control, customer problems, technical product failures, and personnel issues. They must struggle with failure and address numerous challenges both instantaneously and simultaneously. As Noam Wasserman (2012: 6), professor of clinical entrepreneurship at the University of Southern California and author of the seminal work *The Founder's Dilemmas*, puts it: Perhaps no business pursuit is messier than creating an organization from scratch."

Startup life is a turbulent roller-coaster ride. And there is no guarantee for success. Startups are by definition vulnerable ventures, and survival in most cases is questionable. It takes guts, passion, perseverance, and a good deal of luck to maneuver a startup to its next stage, out of the danger zone. Startup founders have to live with manifold frustrations – e.g., an often rigorous career break, the permanent search for additional funding, the likelihood of having to drastically change the startup business model – and they must have the mental strength and energy to face a highly uncertain future. Startup founders need to anticipate basic business dilemmas, avoid sneaky pitfalls, take calculated risks, and cope with chaos, ambiguity, and unpredictability. They must be willing to put in long hours, to live on a minimal income, to accept painful mistakes, and to deal with pressure from family and peer groups.

Startup life is no walk in the park, that much is certain. Accelerators' role in making the walk easier should not be overestimated, but they can help in addressing startup impasses and problems in a more structured way.

There seems to be a growing general consensus in Silicon Valley that startups need a team of founders rather than solo entrepreneurs. Teams are generally better equipped to meet startup dilemmas (Wasserman 2012). Only strong teams will win, so runs the prevailing new venture leadership diagnosis. I attended a closed Silicon Valley investor meeting in which startups pitched for angel funding, and the main criterion used by investors was whether the new business was led by a strong team of passionate founders with convincing entrepreneurial competences, the right mindset, synergy, and determination. For that matter, solo founders were not even taken into consideration for funding. The focus on teams accentuates how important complementary skill sets of startup founder teams are considered (Cohan 2012; Lazear 2004; Lewis 2012; Szycher 2015).[33]

Teams need to have the right mix of product development knowhow (upstream innovation) and product marketing and sales abilities (downstream innovation). In his review of entrepreneurial teams, Thomas Lechler (2001: 276) concludes that "overall the main argument for the advantage of teams is based on the positive effect of a combination of people with different personalities, characteristics, knowledge, skills, and abilities." Startup founder teams are good for emotional support, for sharing and handling business setbacks, for bringing in other perspectives, for adding realism, and for filling skill gaps. One could also point to the wider psychological significance of the startup team's mission. As Katzenbach & Smith (1993: 178) argue: "credible team purposes have an element related to winning, being first, revolutionizing, or being on the cutting edge."

Startup teams need to be goal-driven and achievement-oriented, focused on the development and marketing of innovations, and making use of the experience, expertise, and skills of team members. Effective startup founding teams have at their disposal collective resources that can be mobilized to guide a startup through its demanding first phases. These team resources go above and beyond team members' individual competences. Some team members are good in the technicalities of product development, some excel in marketing, and others know how to set up the startup as a business organization. Startup teams that lack these resources and complementary skills are doomed to fail. Research has shown that the malfunctioning of startup teams is among the main reasons why startups go down (Wasserman 2012). Weak teams will lose. Team building, therefore, is a common activity in accelerator programs.

Talent is Silicon Valley's main resource. This is true for both existing high-tech companies and for startups. Its talented workforce is *the* trademark of the Valley, which enables its continual development of innovative technologies. Talent is a startup's human capital and is responsible for its innovation record, business performance, and growth potential. Surrounded by some of the best universities in the world, Silicon Valley has direct access to a large and renewable pool of talents. Silicon Valley thrives on talented software programmers, coders, engineers, and computer scientists. They are the cement of the Valley as a perpetual and self-reinforcing innovation machine. Talented employees are of paramount importance in the innovation chain from idea generation – via idea elaboration – to marketable new products and services.

A flourishing high-tech startup economy is unthinkable without a highly educated and highly skilled workforce. But high-tech talent Silicon-Valley style is not just about excellence in hard skills such as coding, programming or hardware design. Talent also comes down to outstanding soft skills: creativity, flexibility, curiosity, passion, an orientation towards achievement, the ability to work in teams, openness, a willingness to share, an entrepreneurial mindset, a pro-customer attitude, being good at networking, being willing to learn, and being focused on personal development. Talent, in other words, is about combining hard *and* soft skills. And it is this combination that makes the difference in an innovation economy. Sometimes bigger companies acquire a startup not because of its product or technology but because of its talent, its team skills – a phenomenon also known as 'acqui-hire'.

Working for a startup is unpredictable and non-routine. Job descriptions are meaningless. "Working for an early-stage startup requires figuring out what your job should be every day, how to accomplish things that have never been done before and when you should throw out everything that's already been done and start over."(COMPASS 2015: 17). High-tech Silicon Valley corporates are involved in a constant struggle to recruit the best talent, and job offers reflect this rugged competition in terms of generous salaries, stock options, employee benefits, and company perks. Employer brand, identity, and culture are also major elements in the way talents evaluate prospective high-tech employers. Laszlo Bock (2015), head of people operations at Google, gives an interesting insight into how this Silicon Valley high-tech giant (which receives over two million applications a year) recruits talent and how it remains a talent powerhouse. His basic work rule regarding hiring talent is: "You want them to fall in love with you" (Block 2015: 97). But love must be mutual. As Facebook CEO Mark Zuckerberg states: "I will only hire someone to work directly for me if I would work for that person."[34]

It is far from easy for startups to compete with high-tech corporates in the Valley in hiring top talents. They cannot offer the same salaries, benefits, and perks. Junior software engineers, for instance, may already start with an annual salary of $100,000 (stock options and bonuses not included).[35] Startups therefore need to approach talent recruitment using different unique selling points: they primarily depend on applicants' drive to stand out in a hectic and dynamic work environment and their desire to share the excitement and satisfaction that growing a startup gives. They target those who enjoy working in a small company and in a small team and who relish the idea of personally contributing to a startup's mission and passion. In short, they seek out talent that is passionate about having an impact in their job, even if it is their first job.

Pivot
Startups fuel the rejuvenation and revitalization of mainstream business developments as they come up with new solutions to pressing problems. But it is a role that takes much effort, pain, and sweat. Most startups fail. The main test is to find a balance between upstream innovation (from idea to product) and downstream innovation (from product to market). Product ideas may be brilliant, but the failure to valorize is the end of every startup. This balance is especially urgent after the first round of funding ('the valley of death'), when startups quickly approach the end of their financial runway (Philips 2013). Not finding a responsive market is disastrous for startups. The difference between failing and pulling through can boil down to how and when a startup decides to launch its product in the market. Value creation, market entry, and product acceptance is what startups are all about. Every startup founding team struggles with aligning upstream and downstream innovation (Bauwen 2012, 2013). It is the alpha and omega of startup life. Or as Ruben Daniëls, Silicon Valley startup founder, neatly summarized:

"A startup is a vessel to find a business model around the technology you are developing."[36]

Bringing a startup product successfully to market is a tedious job. First-time startup founders often lack the skill set and experience to make an effective transition from idea to market. Accelerators can be very instrumental in helping startup teams to find their way through the numerous pitfalls of commercialization. Mentorship by experienced serial entrepreneurs can prevent startup founders from making the most common business development mistakes.

Pivoting is a matter of life or death for startups in their effort to survive the early stages as new ventures. It is an important buzzword in the Silicon Valley business glossary. Pivoting directly affects the necessity of balancing upstream and downstream innovation. Endless product polishing is sure to result in startup death, as its funding runway tends to be much too short. Startup founders, to paraphrase renowned Silicon Valley entrepreneurs and authors Reid Hoffman and Ben Casnocha, need to be in "permanent beta".[37] To timely pivot one's business concept should be the prevailing startup logic. "Fail fast", so the Silicon Valley acclaimed motto goes, as that would be better than spending endless amounts of time on product refinement under uncertain conditions of market interest.

This line of thought is convincingly argued by Eric Ries, noted Silicon Valley entrepreneur and author, in *The Lean Startup* (2011). The book is an authoritative combination of analytical guidelines, methodological templates, and practical principles that go beyond startup founders' entrepreneurial instincts. It is clearly one of the most popular books among starting entrepreneurs. The number one insight that Ries puts forth is that "learning is the essential unit for startups" (2011: 49). His Lean Startup Model is based on what is called the Build-Measure-Learn feedback loop. This analytic tool comes down to building a minimum viable product (MVP) with the lowest amount of time, money, and effort. As quickly as possible, the startup team needs to launch the product and meticulously measure basics such as customer reaction, traction profiles, product use, and willingness to pay. This feedback information is used for immediate product alterations and business plan changes. The secret is not to endlessly polish and re-polish a product but to market the product in its early stage, to monitor customer take-up and feedback, and to process this information through pivoting product adjustments. "If we're not moving the drivers of our business model, we're not making progress. That becomes a sure sign that it's time to pivot." (ibid.: 120).

Within a remarkably short period, the term "pivot" became a leading concept in Silicon Valley's startup vocabulary. The merits of Ries' approach are twofold. First, it is counterintuitive. The idea is not to develop the perfect product, because if that fails it will surely mark the end of the startup given that it was simply incapable of meeting consumers' needs. The idea is to quickly launch an MVP and use customer reaction to change the initial product and to make a better product-market fit. While the MVP is still full of bugs, it is shipped to customers way before it is market-ready in traditional business terms. For strongly product-driven startup entrepreneurs, pivoting is often an agonizing experience – a nightmare, even – as they believe in their product and because it took great persever-ance to build it. The pain is not so much in building the MVP but in *not* building the ideal product. Fortunately, Ries offers a variety of practical suggestions on how and when to pivot. The second merit of his approach is the emphasis on solid quantitative measurements of customer feedback and product use. Ries' methodology is firmly data-based, and collecting primary metrics on customer response and take-up is seen as a startup's core activity.

The need to pivot is based on a commitment to iterations that is being fed by repeated MVP testing, customer accounting, product alteration experimentation, progress measuring – or, as Ries calls it, "validated learn-ing" (ibid.: 18-19). Startups operate under conditions of extreme uncertainty, and the trick is to make the right choice between persisting or pivoting, between continuing on the current path or making a sharp turn.[38] Effec-tive pivoting mirrors startups' resilience and agility. It takes guts to pivot, and the principle of validated learning may improve a startup's survival chances. One of the distinct roles of accelerators, as will become clear, is helping startups with timely pivoting, as this is what makes or breaks a startup.

The meso level: Capital, universities, government, and support networks

The Silicon Valley ecosystem facilitates startup founders in building their new businesses through an advanced network of institutional facilitators and resources: angel and VC investors (startup funding), universities and research centers (talent pool and knowledge), government (innovation policy, technology funding, visa), and the startup support infrastructure (accelerators, legal advice). I briefly outline how these institutional pillars of the Silicon Valley ecosystem have enabled the region to become and remain the global epicenter of innovation and high-tech startups.

Startup funding: Angels and VCs

Funding, obviously, is of paramount significance for startups. Or, in the more prosaic words of Silicon Valley analyst Tapan Munroe: "Ideas are the soul of innovation, money is the life blood." (2009: 72). Money from friends, family, and fools is a welcome but also a vulnerable source of startup financing. Access to professional investors – i.e., to angel and VC funding – is another pillar of Silicon Valley's advanced ecosystem. Crowdfunding is becoming more important, too. Startup funding has been around for a long time in the Valley and has indisputably added to the strength of its innovation economy and new venture entrepreneurship. Recent data show that half of all U.S. venture capital is invested in Silicon Valley companies, more than all other U.S. regions combined.[39] The Valley even attracts over 15% of total *global* VC funding. No other region in the world captures such a high share of domestic and foreign venture capital. Between 2009 and 2014, VC firms invested over $31 billion in Silicon Valley companies.[40] Particularly relevant sectors are software, biotechnology, clean technology, and health.

Sand Hill Road in Menlo Park is a legendary address, as it houses the highest concentration of prominent VC companies. One of them is Sequoia Capital, founded in 1972 and among the most well-known VC firms, having funded such illustrious high-tech companies as Apple, Atari, Cisco, Oracle, Google, Yahoo, YouTube, LinkedIn, PayPal, WhatsApp, Airbnb, and Instagram. The total funds raised by Sequoia amount to $4.12 billion; and it has overseen 57 IPOs, 170 acquisitions, and 1,235 investments in almost 700 companies.[41] In 2014, it participated in the selling of WhatsApp to Facebook for a staggering $19 billion, which made it the largest acquisition in the history of a venture-backed company at the time. Kleiner, Perkins, Caufield & Byers (KPCB), whose offices are next door to Sequoia on Sand Hill Road, is another major Silicon Valley VC (also founded in 1972) with $2.68 billion of funds raised, 41 IPOs, 112 acquisitions, and 836 investments in over 450 companies.[42] KPCB was involved in funding AOL, Citrix, Compaq, Lotus, Symantec, Genentech, Zynga, Amazon, and Twitter, to name just a few companies. These figures on funding and exits substantiate CB Insights' conclusion that "it is clear that the Silicon Valley tech hub is the 800 lb. gorilla when it comes to both venture-backed tech financing and exit activity."[43] Other premium Silicon Valley VC funds include Andreessen & Horowitz, Benchmark Ventures, Khosla Ventures, New Enterprise Associates, Accel, and Greylock.

Public and private pension funds, university endowments, and foundations are among the largest U.S. institutional VC funders. Commercial banks play a minor role. Former banker John Dean has a straightforward explanation for this: "The prevailing culture of banks, particularly large ones, is risk-aversive; it isn't quite suited to the freewheeling, risk-embracing ethos of Silicon Valley."[44] The investment logic of banks and VCs differs markedly.

Venture capital is big in Silicon Valley, but so is startup funding demand. It takes serious capital to run a startup, and there are thousands of Silicon Valley startups competing for funding, among them a large cohort of non-U.S. startups that settle in the Valley to raise VC funding. Building and growing a startup in Silicon Valley is expensive, as the cost of living is high and recruiting highly skilled staff is very costly. A startup's financial runway is short, and its cash burn rate is generally high. Most startups do not succeed in raising sufficient capital to grow their business. The majority fails, and only the best survive. Silicon Valley's definition of 'the best', as I outlined above, is based on two criteria: scalability and growth potential. That is why VCs are more interested in later-stage funding, when startups have matured and are able to show market traction. VCs are predominantly looking for what they call a 'hockey stick' growth curve: a revenue curve that takes an initial linear (slow) growth rate but then suddenly turns into an exponential (much faster) growth curve (Philips 2013). The mobile devices and apps sectors are big game changers in this respect.

VC investments are high-risk investments, and VCs consequently aim for high returns on their money. One big winner compensates for the losses on many other startup investments. VC startup investment math is not rocket science, is highly intuitive, and according to *Forbes* contributor Bruce Booth, "a big part of the problem is that anecdotal stories about great returns drive much of the thinking."[45] Only successful startups will survive; the ones that fail but also received funding simply disappear from the radar. Picking a winner remains the greatest VC challenge, as is keeping the valuation of fast-growing businesses realistic given the recent fear of an implosion of overpriced and overhyped unicorn startups (CB Insights 2016; Wadhwa 2016).[46] VCs are also competitors in the sense that they are all searching for the next startup champion, the one that will generate their multiple returns on investment (ROI). It could create an investors' tragedy of the commons. The fear of missing out –commonly abbreviated as FOMO –may override a VC's fear of losing money, as Silicon Valley investor Bill Gurley, partner at Benchmark, has warned.[47]

How does the VC business works? Investments in new ventures begin with a pre-seed stage (family, friends) and move on to the seed stage, the early stage, the expansion stage, and later stages. In technical terms, these stages are known as series Seed, series A, series B, series C, series D+. The more mature the startup stage, the higher the VC investment – depending, of course, on the startup's capital intensity and valuation. Series Seed is the stage in which ideas and products are developed; the funding of this stage is typically between $250,000 and $750,000. Series A is about optimizing product and user base; the funding at this stage ranges between $3 million and $6 million. Series B is for expanding market reach; the funding varies between $6 million to more than $15 million. Series C and later is used for scaling; funding ranges from single digits and double digits to hundreds of millions, or even billions. Uber raised over $10 billion (series G), and Airbnb over $3.4 billion (series F). The later the investment stage, the more important the hockey stick return on investment calculus becomes. Huge investments are at stake. Series C, D, and E are later-stage investments that are usually aimed at working towards an exit, either via a trade sale or an IPO. VCs demand a greater say in these later investment rounds, which may involve drastic changes in the startup team, as growing a startup requires different skills than launching a startup.

Angel investors are more active in early-stage startup funding. They typically are successful former entrepreneurs with considerable business experience and extensive networks who like to invest their private money in startups. Angels are appreciated by startup founders for providing them with 'smart money': the combination of cash, expertise, experience, time, mentorship, and valuable contacts and networks. This is probably the greatest advantage of the Silicon Valley funding support system. Investing in startups is not simply a matter of providing capital ('dumb money') to lengthen a new venture's runway. It is also a matter of investing smart money, and many startup founders will admit that this helped enormously to make them stronger and to bring their new business to the next level. Smart money counts.

Silicon Valley accelerators have strong relationships with VCs; there is a clear understanding of mutual dependency and shared benefits. Accelerators bring VCs into contact with promising startups, and VCs get direct access to startup teams they may want to invest in. And in many cases, accelerators are backed by VC funds, which permit an even more direct role and active participation.

Talent pool and knowledge: Universities and research labs
Higher education is an indispensable institution in an advanced pro-innovation and pro-startup ecosystem. Surrounded by some of the best universities and research labs in the world, Silicon Valley has a gold mine of talent, innovation, and knowledge.[48] The Bay Area is home to the University

of California with its four campuses (Berkeley, San Francisco, Davis, and Santa Cruz), Stanford University in the heart of Silicon Valley (Palo Alto), California State University with its two campuses (San Francisco and San Jose), and Santa Clara University.[49]

Berkeley (a public university) and Stanford (a private university) are two of the most renowned institutions for higher learning inside and outside the U.S., and both top all major national and international academic rankings. No less than 29 Nobel prizes have been awarded to Berkeley alumni, while Stanford has 32 faculty members who have received this most prestigious academic honor. Altogether, the Bay Area universities enroll about 175,000 students, a quarter of whom are graduate students. The area is furthermore served by a widely branched network of California Community Colleges, which are core feeders of the region's universities. The Foothill-De Anza Community College District, located in central Silicon Valley, enrolls about 65,000 students (one of whom was Steve Jobs). Such large numbers of students provide a continuous and abundant supply of highly skilled talent that Silicon Valley's high-tech firms and startups are eager to recruit from. The Bay Area universities provide outstanding training at all educational levels. Moreover, they coach thousands of PhD students working on specialized dissertation projects that add to their educational excellence and state-of-the-art research quality. The great reputation of the Bay Area's universities means that they are able to hire the best and brightest academics, which further strengthens educational and research quality. The Bay Area is a magnet for not only startup founders but also students and academics.

But the area's innovation ecosystem is not just tied to universities. There are numerous public and private, independent and corporate, federal and state R&D institutes and labs that all add to the innovation standing of this premier high-tech region. Some of the more well-known of these are Lawrence Berkeley National Laboratory, Lawrence Livermore National Laboratory, Sandia National Laboratories, SLAC National Accelerator Laboratory, NASA Ames Research Center, Joint Genome Institute, SRI International, PARC, California Institute for Regenerative Medicine, Buck Institute for Research on Ageing, Ernest Gallo Clinic and Research Center, Joint BioEnergy Institute, and, of course, the various corporate in-house R&D laboratories (Bay Area Council 2012). These exceptional universities, research institutes, and laboratories attract the best researchers from all over the world and pull in substantial external innovation and research funds. For academics in the top league, the Bay Area cannot be matched in terms of its innovation environment, providing them with a place to pursue their career, work with their peers, teach smart and dedicated students, and enjoy the challenge of a competitive ambiance. And to top it all off, the weather is not bad either.

The Silicon Valley innovation and startup ecosystem goes beyond the mere existence of world-class universities and extends to the way universities collaborate with high-tech industry and encourage entrepreneurship among its faculty and students. One thing the Bay Area universities cannot be accused of is being focused on ivory-tower research. For decades, they have had a strong entrepreneurial mindset and have developed close cooperative relationships with industry. The commercialization of research output is high on the universities' agenda, which underlines the role of applied knowledge, of finding innovative solutions to practical problems, and of working together with industrial stakeholders. This symbiotic university-industry collaboration is highly cherished. Industry participates in the university, and universities for their part reach out to industry. As Emilio Castilla et al. (2000: 229) conclude: "The educational sector has been especially vital because the constant movement back and forth between industry and university has blurred the boundaries of both and created elaborate social networks that keep academic research focused on practical problems, and infuse industrial activity with up-to-date science." Professors are stimulated to valorize their research on innovations, and universities often have special arrangements for faculty and students to launch their own startups. A legendary Stanford example is Hewlett-Packard, which was founded by two Stanford graduates in the late 1930s and coached by the brilliant Stanford Dean Frederick Terman. Hewlett-Packard has since grown into an electronics behemoth with over 300,000 employees and revenues of more than $110 billion.[50]

Bay Area universities encourage the founding of startups, and the record of accomplishment is remarkable. Pioneering startups that were founded by Berkeley graduates and alumni include great names such as Intel, Apple, Sybase, Oracle, Sun Microsystems, Gap, and early biotechnology companies such as Chiron Corporation, Tularik, Exelixis, and Renovis. Calculations show that companies founded by Berkeley faculty, graduates, and alumni employ over half a million people and have annual revenues over $315 billion.[51] Since 1990, over 145 new ventures have been launched under the umbrella of Berkeley's IP licenses. SkyDeck is Berkeley's first startup accelerator, located in a 10,000 square-foot space. It works with corporate partners and has launched over 70 startups.[52]

Stanford can also pride itself on a fabulous startup history. Eesley & Miller (2012) have calculated that almost 40,000 active companies are Stanford spinoffs, which together produce annual revenues of $2.7

trillion and 5.4 million jobs. Among them are illustrious companies such as Hewlett-Packard, Google, Nike, Cisco, Sun, Yahoo, VMware, PayPal, LinkedIn, Netflix, and Tesla. The authors conclude that "if these companies collectively formed an independent nation, its estimated economy would be the world's 10th largest." (ibid.: 7). The economic, social, and cultural impact of companies started by Stanford faculty, students, and alumni goes beyond the imagination. In 2010, the top 150 Silicon Valley companies that were Stanford-affiliated had a total market capitalization of $650 billion and sales totaling about $270 billion.[53]

Both Stanford and Berkeley promote startup founding through a wide array of resources, services, and networks: student mentoring and coaching; access to funding, patents and IPs; technology licensing; financial faculty incentives; special entrepreneurship courses; incubators and accelerators; extracurricular programs; leadership and team training; strategy and pivoting courses; internships at the Valley's high-tech corporates; and startup innovation and funding competitions (Ester & Maas 2016: 145-154). Berkeley, for instance, is known for its Haas School of Business entrepreneurship programs and the Fung Institute for Engineering Leadership. Stanford excels through its Stanford Technology Ventures Program (STVP), which focuses on the acceleration of high-tech entrepreneurship. In these programs, alumni entrepreneurs always play a major role as mentor and coach and also offer student internships.

A closer look at the curricula of the Bay Area higher education institutions reveals that developing entrepreneurial skills and a pro-entrepreneurship attitude is a structural feature of basically *all* courses. Creativity, innovation, sharing, thinking big, problem solving, and competitiveness are standard components of the curriculum. The universities provide a learning and experimenting environment in which students are encouraged to start their own businesses, to become entrepreneurs. They help them to turn their idea into a marketable product and supply them with the necessary resources. Bay Area universities (and research labs) show a unique combination of academic excellence and entrepreneurship. This double mindset has made the area into a highly successful innovation and startup region. It has created an entrepreneurial culture that blends both innovation-mindedness and innovation valorization, and upstream and downstream innovation.[54]

Silicon Valley's rich talent pool is a major competitive advantage and a solid pillar of its ecosystem. But the talent pool must be maintained regularly in order for high-tech companies and startups to continue prospering in the near future. There are serious indications that in view of the drastic budget cuts in recent years, the California system of public higher learning needs a significant investment upgrade (Public Policy Institute of California 2015; Bay Area Council 2012, 2014a, 2016). Its reputation appears to be at stake.

Facilitating government

Many American high-tech entrepreneurs tend to believe that technological innovation should be left to free market forces and that government should not interfere with their business. The role of government in innovation development, they argue, is and should be minimal. In my view, this prevalent opinion is based on a myth that needs serious debunking, as it is at odds with American innovation and technology policy over the last seventy years. The U.S. government has, in fact, played a pivotal role in building strong ecosystems such as Silicon Valley. The history of Silicon Valley clearly shows that the U.S. government has been a prime mover in promoting technological innovation: through massive R&D funding, as a first customer of innovations, in its regulation of market rules, and in its facilitation of high-tech talent. High-tech companies, including new ventures, have greatly profited from this active government intervention.

World War I led to a spike in the U.S. navy's demand for more powerful radio technology for its war fleet, which spawned the development of more reliable and more advanced shipboard transmitters and transmitter stations. FTC, a Stanford 'startup', was the first Bay Area company to develop vacuum tube technology and was awarded large government contracts. It marked the start of a flourishing radio technology industry in the region. World War II and the Korean War accelerated the demand for high-frequency radar and worldwide networks of radio communications systems. The U.S. government quickly became the prime contractor for commissioning military research and the funder of innovative defense technologies (e.g., microwave technology). This burgeoning military demand for high-tech radar and communications systems gave a formidable boost to the development of the Bay Area's R&D and led to the founding of pioneering research centers.

The Cold War resulted in an unprecedented technological rivalry between the U.S. and the Soviet Union, leading to a furious Space Race between the two power blocs. This prompted the Bay Area to enter a new sector of technological innovation: aerospace and missiles. The region greatly benefited from the massive government defense spending at the height of the Cold War, which helped to create an advanced and highly competitive innovation-based ecosystem. Without these unprecedented levels of defense expenditure, Silicon Valley would not be what it is today. As historian Stuart Leslie (2000: 49) concludes: "For better and for worse, Silicon Valley owes its present configuration to patterns of federal spending, corporate strategies, industry-university relationships, and technological innovation shaped by the assumptions and priorities of Cold War defense policy."

The technological developments before and early after World War II helped to build an innovation infrastructure that became a fertile basis for the semiconductor revolution that transformed Silicon Valley into the main region in the U.S. for manufacturing silicon devices. This is what gave the Valley its name, and this in turn prepared Silicon Valley for the next revolution, which gave way to the PC era and, later, the software explosion. The Valley became a vibrant place of pioneering technological innovation in which universities, high-tech companies, and research centers greatly benefited from the U.S. government as a driving force of innovation. As the Bay Area Science & Innovation Consortium Report concludes: "No other region in the United States or in the world has more federally funded research centers and laboratories."[55] For example, over 80% of Stanford University's more than 5,300 externally sponsored projects (totaling $1.33 billion in 2014-2015) is funded by federal money.[56]

The stereotype of a passive U.S. government in the technological domain is not justified and needs to be demystified. It is rhetoric rather than fact. The U.S. government did and does play a leading role in the development, diffusion, and adoption of technological innovations. Mariana Mazzucato convincingly reasons in her book, *The Entrepreneurial State*, that: "Despite the perception of the U.S. as the epitome of private sector-led wealth crea-tion, in reality it is the State that has been engaged on a massive scale in entrepreneurial risk-taking to spur innovation. (...) The insight gained is that other than being an entrepreneurial society, a place where it is culturally natural to start and grow a business, the U.S. is also a place where the State plays an entrepreneurial role, by making investments in radical new areas." (Mazzucato 2014: 73). The Apple iPhone, the iPod, and the iPad, she shows, make use of innovative technologies that were funded by federal and military U.S. R&D programs. These smart technologies are the products of decades of government investments in fundamental and applied innovation research.

But the role of the U.S. government goes further than massive funding of innovative technologies and R&D. It has also acted as a launching customer of technologies and innovations, as a lawmaker, as a simulator of small business participation, and as a supplier of visas for foreign workers. Of particular importance was the Bayh-Dole Act of 1980 that regulated the transfer of property rights of federally funded research to the university or the research laboratory through the design of a uniform patent policy. This new system of property rights spurred the commercialization of new technologies, innovations, and knowledge that were acquired via government-funded projects. The 1981 R&D tax credit law helped companies to finance basic research and development activities. The Small Business Innovation Research (SBIR) program of 1982 was instrumental in supporting SMEs to qualify for early-stage funding and to help them through the tough first stages of the innovation cycle, allowing them to bridge the feared 'valley of death'.

Immigrants play a major role in Silicon Valley's ecosystem, both as startup founders and as high-tech workers. Allocating quotas for immigrants was and remains a tricky business and a much debated issue. The Hart-Celler Act of 1965 changed the way the U.S. government set quotas from one based on an immigrant's national origin to one that gives preference to immigrants with specialized skills and is still intact today. It led to a radical increase in the number of talented immigrants, though many Silicon Valley entrepreneurs feel that the procedure itself remains a long and often frustrating process. Especially H-1B visas (for non-U.S. scientists with a 'specialty occupation') are a source of chagrin among startup founders who want to hire foreign specialists, as demand greatly exceeds supply. The Trump administration has announced that it would review the quota policy as part of its 'buy American, hire American' doctrine.

These four examples illustrate that the U.S. federal government has played an active role in stimulating innovation and in 'regulating' the innovation market. It has provided the startup business community with a sense of long-term stability and predictability (with the exception of some visa regulations). More recently, the Obama administration introduced the 2012 JOBS (Jumpstart Our Business Startups) Act, which enables startups to raise funding among the general public and not just among accredited investors. The new law, according to Silicon Valley author Randall Stross (2012: 205), demonstrates that "startups, as a category, had become darlings in Washington".

Startup support infrastructure: Accelerators and legal advice
Silicon Valley and networking have always gone hand in hand. Entrepreneurship is embedded in a professional regional system of business support and counseling. Accelerators are a vital part of this network support system because they offer resources to startup teams to build, scale, and grow their new venture. These resources (coaching, mentoring, training, funding, networks) are exactly why accelerators are given such a prominent place in my Silicon Valley Innovation and Startup Model. But there are

other actors and agencies in the support system that also exist to service startups. The Valley's ecosystem offers access to lawyers, accountants, domain experts, and, as described above, angels and VCs, all of whom help startup founders to refine, develop, and commercialize their business. The ecosystem consists of extensive social networks that link startups to corporates, investors, talent, (potential) customers, and stakeholders (Castilla et al. 2000). Networking by startup founders can create new business opportunities, new market venues, new partnerships, and new deals. Networking, according to Van Weele (2016), is the main mechanism through which accelerators contribute to startup achievement: "Networking enables startups to access missing resources, to efficiently acquire market, business and technological knowledge, to gain legitimacy, to overcome challenges in the entrepreneurial ecosystem and to raise investments." (2016: 213). And as I outline in the next section, networking also has a cultural component: it is part of the Valley's entrepreneurial spirit, its social mindset, its business mind.

Law firms play a distinct role in the Valley's startup economy and network support system. Unlike mainstream European law practices, they not only offer legal expertise on how to start a new venture but also provide tailor-made business advice. Law firms assist startups in their early-stage business development by opening doors to investors, corporate stakeholders, and possible partners. They offer contacts and introductions that startup founders need. "It is often a lawyer's ability to make a key introduction to a potential source of funds or corporate partner that a beginning entrepreneur values most." (Johnson 2000: 327). Law firms first and foremost help startups with the legal paperwork and technicalities that setting up a new venture entails, but their role is much broader in assisting beginning entrepreneurs. Their advice may concern startup structure, management issues, team formation, financing, staff hiring, business strategy and proof of concept, stock ownership, patents, tax matters, etc. Lawyers help startup founders in addressing dilemmas and pitfalls typically encountered by new ventures. In this sense, they are more business advisers than legal consultants. According to sociologist Mark Suchman (2000), Silicon Valley lawyers serve as dealmakers, counselors, gatekeepers, proselytizers, and matchmakers. They are a startup's *consigliere*.[57] And the legal market is sizeable in Silicon Valley. Weinberg & Heine (2014) have calculated that there are over 400 law firms and nearly 3,000 attorneys in Palo Alto alone (roughly one lawyer per twenty residents).

An interesting feature of the active involvement of Silicon Valley lawyers in mentoring startup teams is that they often work on the basis of the pay-it-forward principle: billing is postponed until startup revenues come in, or law firms (and sometimes individual lawyers) may take stock ownership in lieu of payment.[58] Such deferred fee arrangements relieve startups in their financially most precarious phase: early-stage development and the 'valley of death' phase in which revenues are still insufficient to cover costs. This payment flexibility means that startups are not deprived of the legal advice they need when launching their new business.

There is a fine line between legal advice, business advice, and entrepreneurship, and as a result, roles often overlap. European law firms generally feel more comfortable with a stricter role definition that separates legal advice from business counseling, and indeed, national legislation in Europe often requires just such a role distinction. Ethical issues may be at stake as well, such as conflicting interests between independent legal advice and private benefits.[59] Lawyers in the Silicon Valley startup ecosystem pursue a broader, more entrepreneurship-based role – a professional self-definition that has made them influential.

As will become clear in the following chapters, accelerators also have a key position in the Silicon Valley network support system, as their mission is to gear up startup teams for launching their new venture in the marketplace and for growing traction and customer reach. Having gone through a high-profile, influential accelerator program provides a startup with credibility and goodwill. And above all: with good funding prospects.

The macro level: Culture, culture, culture

Silicon Valley has an amazing innovation ecosystem that is based on a number of powerful institutions, as I have outlined in this chapter. But this is only part of the success narrative. Equally important is that the Valley is characterized by a shared culture that embraces innovation and applauds entrepreneurship – a culture that has inspired generations of startup founders who have combined passion and ambition to create some of the world's most imaginative high-tech companies. The Valley has a pulsating startup culture and business community that has a magic appeal to new venture founders. Newcomers to the area can almost feel the vibe, the stream of positive energy blended with a can-do mentality. To a certain degree, this reflects the typical American West Coast frontier state of mind, but the Valley appears to magnify this cultural temperament.

The open communication mode and the willingness to share ideas and innovations are among the most striking cultural traits of Silicon Valley's startup community. It always fascinates me how frankly startup founders talk about their new business concept: the product, underlying technology, business model, market potential, investors, growth challenges, strengths and weaknesses of their startup, etc. There seems to be no fear of giving away business 'secrets'. This open attitude is one that many European observers find difficult to understand but usually greatly admire. Startup founders are willing to share their business idea but in return expect feedback, even when their idea is in a very embryonic and vulnerable stage. Sharing can strengthen your own ideas – this seems to be the prevailing cultural message. You do not 'sit' on your business concept, as the mainstream European response tends to be, fearing that competitors might run off with your idea.

This open communication style is refreshing: it activates innovation feedback, generates new leads, and triggers self-reflection and learning. As Chong Moon-Lee and his co-authors observe: "The prevailing business philosophy promotes openness, learning, sharing of information, the co-evolution of ideas, flexibility, mutual feedback, and fast responses to opportunities and challenges."[60] Networking is an essential part of this welcoming business philosophy, as new contacts may produce new business prospects. Everybody is willing to grant you time, even if it is only five minutes, to outline your startup business idea. It is one of the most pleasing qualities of the Valley's business culture.

The entrepreneurial attitude that colors the micro-level of startup creation discussed earlier in this chapter mirrors the culture of Silicon Valley entrepreneurship at the aggregate level, a culture that emphasizes the need to think big, to launch disruptive technologies, to change the world, and to go for moonshots (projects that address a huge problem, propose a radical solution, and use breakthrough technology). In the Valley, one encounters grand cultural narratives articulated in grand Silicon Valley jargon. One of the most spectacular examples is Elon Musk's plan to colonize Mars and turn the human race into a multi-planetary species – an incredible business adventure that is beyond the human imagination but an adventure that his company SpaceX is nonetheless seriously working on. Its mission is "to revolutionize space technology with the ultimate goal of enabling people to live on other planets."[61] This is thinking big to the max.

Risk-taking and the tolerance of failure are among the most defining features of Silicon Valley's business culture, which directly impact the startup economy. Risk proneness is seen as a positive trait that makes up the psychological core of entrepreneurial thinking and acting. The prevailing maxim is: no risk, no glory. The acceptance of failure is another compelling Silicon Valley cultural phenomenon. Startup founders who fail are not confronted with the common negative stereotypes that often mark the European reaction towards new venture failure and bankruptcy. The stigmatization of starting entrepreneurs who fail is not part of the Valley's business culture.[62] Entrepreneurs frankly discuss why their startup was unsuccessful and the lessons they learned for building a new venture.[63] A failed startup is a meaningful learning experience, and VCs even favor startup entrepreneurs who have prior experience with a startup that did not make it. Failure, of course, remains a painful event and is not admired for its own sake. As Reid Hoffman, LinkedIn's co-founder, noted: "We don't celebrate failure in Silicon Valley. We celebrate learning." Startup failure in Silicon Valley does not equal personal failure. The fact that the tolerance of failure is high also adds to a business climate that is optimistic and self-confident. It has to be underlined that, unlike most European countries, U.S. legislation (e.g., bankruptcy laws, limited partnerships) is such that it limits personal liability for startup founders and their investors. It is easier to close down a company. Studies indicate that more lenient bankruptcy laws positively affect self-employment as well as firm entry and exit rates (Armour & Cumming 2008; Fan & White 2003; Cerqueiro et al. 2017).

Silicon Valley's business economy never stops; it runs 24/7. Its work attitude is unmatched. Building a startup requires unconditional attention and permanent availability, as you must develop products that will shake markets, find new customers, pivot, address the many problems that startups have to face, and stay ahead of the competition. The drive to excel pervades the Valley's startup community and creates a business culture of passionate and committed entrepreneurship. Hard work, perseverance, and giving your all are the rule for both startup founders and their employees. It is a work culture characterized by an all-or-nothing attitude. Heated debates on work-life balance are rare. Complaining about long hours is 'uncool'; building a startup is not a picnic. Startup stress is definitely prevalent in Silicon Valley, but it is not a conversation topic. Yu-Kuan Lin, co-founder of Everyday.me and a Y Combinator graduate, once said: "Nothing prepares you for founding a startup besides founding a startup." (Deering 2014: 137).

But even all the hard work in the world cannot prevent the fact that most startups fail, even in Silicon Valley. CB Insights (2014) investigated the main reasons for startup failure by analyzing data from over 100 startup failure post-mortems. The top seven causes, in descending order, are: no market need for product, running out of cash, wrong team, being outcompeted, pricing/cost issues, poor product, or lack of a business model.[64] "Fail fast, fail often" is a much-heard Silicon Valley aphorism that refers to the need for timely startup closing in order to avoid what VCs call 'the walking dead': startups that go on too long without any serious revenue.

Diversity is a cherished goal in Silicon Valley. It is believed that a highly diverse workforce in terms of ethnicity, gender, and nationality is good for innovation. It brings multiple perspectives, challenging viewpoints, out-of-the-box thinking, and global frames of reference, and it broadens the talent pool. High-tech companies operate worldwide and therefore need a diverse workforce to understand and service global customers (Hunt et al. 2015). Though the big high-tech Silicon Valley corporations nourish the ideal of diversity, their workforces still show considerable ethnic and gender biases (Ester & Maas 2016: 125-129). There is still a world to win: African-Americans, Latinos, and women are underrepresented, while whites and Asians are overrepresented.

A clear diversity asset of the Valley is the number of highly successful immigrant entrepreneurs. One out of two new ventures in Silicon Valley is started by immigrants, which is twice as high as the U.S. average. The total market capitalization of venture-backed U.S. companies founded by immigrants totals $900 billion, and they employ about 600,000 people.[65]

Culture matters in Silicon Valley. It is a determining factor in explaining why the region thrives on innovation and entrepreneurship, why it succeeded in becoming and remaining a global paradise for high-tech startups. Silicon Valley's ecosystem flourishes because it is backed by a cultural mindset that is highly competitive, willing to take risks, passionate about entrepreneurship, achievement-oriented, and driven by the need to make a difference in the world. Accelerators, as I will show in the following chapters, explicitly address the importance of working on a startup mindset that matches the Silicon Valley way of thinking and takes advantage of its omnipresent entrepreneurial culture.

In this chapter, I have analyzed Silicon Valley's ecosystem and the way it perpetuates innovation and feeds startup creation. Understanding this ecosystem is necessary for comprehending the role of accelerators in the Valley. It provides the bigger picture that is necessary for assessing how accelerators empower startup teams to build and grow their new businesses.

3   Unique Selling Points

Accelerator Philosophy, Business Model, and Cooperation

I start my analysis of the 23 accelerators that I interviewed by examining their founders' core philosophy on coaching startups and helping them scale and grow, the variety in the scope and focus of accelerators' programs, their business model, and the way they collaborate with external partners in Silicon Valley. Some accelerators, as we will see, have a general scope, whereas others focus on specific technologies or niche markets. Some accelerators accept large numbers of startups, whereas others prefer to be small. This difference in focus and size corresponds with differences in accelerator coaching programs. It also relates to two distinct accelerator business models: profit versus non-profit objectives.

To help us in analyzing the data in this study, I make a distinction between two types of accelerators. The first consists of general/low-touch accelerators that are quite large, cover a wide range of technologies, and offer cohort-based programs. The other type comprises specialized/high-touch accelerators that operate in distinct markets and coach a limited number of startup teams but on a very intensive basis. It must be emphasized that "low-touch" is meant in a relative sense – i.e., compared to the intensive, personalized, and longer coaching period of high-touch accelerators. This distinction is similar to the four accelerator types mentioned by CBIA (2016). The CBIA study developed an accelerator matrix with two axes – focus and resources – which results in four accelerator types: intense/general; intense/focused; light/general; light/focused. The general vs. focused dimension refers to the nature of the accelerator's technology domain, whereas the intense vs. light dimension addresses the magnitude of the accelerator's support resources.

But first we must look at what separates an incubator from an accelerator. I posed this question to my sample of accelerator executives.

Incubators versus accelerators

In the first chapter I outlined a number of criteria that conceptually differentiate accelerators from incubators: entry, duration, funding, program intensity, teams, culture, and cohorts. It was emphasized that these differences are gradual, and that in practice incubators and accelerators show considerable overlap (Bay Area Council Economic Institute 2016). In fact, one may even argue that accelerators are advanced, next-phase incubators. The two growth models are ideal types – theoretical constructions – that cannot be observed in their purest form. Reality, as I will show, demonstrates less robustness and more heterogeneity. Several accelerator executives accentuate this variance in growth model functions and options, though elementary differences are clearly recognized. A majority of executives point out that incubators focus on very early-stage business ideas, whereas the primary goal of accelerators is to grow new ventures that already have a product, a business model, and even some traction. As Prem Talreja, vice president of marketing at The Fabric, explains: "Incubators offer limited but essential support: a little amount of money, office space, and infrastructure. It's like a hotel. (...) Accelerators help you succeed by putting in management support, by giving you access to customers, by creating events where customers come in, and get yourself exposed to the marketplace. (...) They have a venture arm." Harm TenHoff, founder and CEO of BayLink (Santa Clara), reiterates this point: "The term incubator is much older than the term accelerator. An incubator is about very early-stage companies or propositions: sometimes there even is no company yet, but just an idea. An accelerator is about companies that have a product, a beginning of a market, but want to accelerate and expand their market." This is further corroborated by Cindy Klein-Marmer, associate director of the Babson College Butler Venture Accelerator Program: "I think in essence you tend to incubate ideas when they are earlier stage and accelerate something that is already up and running." Naomi Kokubo, co-founder and COO of Founders Space, agrees: "An incubator helps teams to redefine their business idea into a real product; an accelerator helps startups to grow their business and bring it to the next step. (...) But a lot of people don't strictly go by this definition."

Quite a number of respondents believe that incubators are first and foremost real-estate-based startup facilitators, whereas accelerators go much further in their support services. Prashant Shah, managing director of TiE LaunchPad, explains: "The primary motivation of incubators early on was to rent or lease office space by the desk, by the cubical. They may offer value-added services, such as access to mentors, investors, and customers. But those are all value-added above and beyond the fact that they are getting rent. Accelerators are not necessarily real estate based. They often provide office space for free for their program participants. Most of them are making money by equity or by a mandatory fee."

Most executives use the terms 'incubator' and 'accelerator' rather loosely. As Brian Hoffman, vice president of revenue and director of legal affairs of

StartX, points out: "The two words have kind of lost meaning. Originally, an incubator is more ideation trying to find fit. An accelerator is a little further down the pipeline: companies already have a business idea, they are looking to scale the idea." Sean Randolph, Silicon Valley expert and senior director of the Bay Area Council Economic Institute, adds that both terms are often used interchangeably and lack clear descriptions. Sean defines incubators as: "The place for very early-stage companies, typically providing some kind of space or facilities, and maybe some mentoring. Accelerators are more often a notch or two more advanced in terms of a resident company's stage development. There may be some kind of direct investment, in return for equity. The level of service may also be more advanced, with more specific advice and support on market development for the company's products, and possibly introductions to investors." Matt Walters, former CEO of the Runway incubator, feels that incubators and accelerators "overlap quite a bit". He notes that: "One of the core differences is that accelerators usually have set a defined period of time in which they are running programs. Three months is more or less the standard. The other thing is we [Runway] are not providing any investment for the companies who are with us, while an accelerator usually comes with an investment."[66]

Accelerators are closer to commercialization and to bringing a startup's product to market. But accelerator mentor and Silicon Valley expert Susan Lucas-Conwell believes that "the lines have really blurred. (...) I would say that the only distinction to be made is that you don't generally have incubators with no office space." Gary Coover, head of global operations at Samsung NEXT, has his own take on the subject: "Truthfully, I think that the distinction between the two has been so convoluted, not just here in the Valley but in all ecosystems, that the issue no longer matters. You can call us an incubator, you can call us a seed fund, you can call us an accelerator, it doesn't really matter. What matters is the value we provide to startups beyond investment dollars."

Core philosophy and focus

What differentiates Silicon Valley accelerators in terms of their mission and target technology? There is a clear distinction between profit and not-for-profit accelerators. The primary goal of the first group is to grow startup companies for investment purposes, and taking equity in promising new ventures is a dominant acquisition strategy. The second group of accelerators are primarily mission-driven and typically focus on creating societal value. The profit-driven larger accelerators are generally based on a high-volume/low-touch business model, while mission-driven accelerators tend to be smaller. It has to be added, however, that the reverse logic does not apply: quite a number of smaller accelerators are profit-driven as well, particularly those that focus on specific technologies. Consequently, the general/low-touch and specialized/high-touch dichotomy does not coincide with this distinction between profit and non-profit business models.

Let's first examine the larger, general/low-touch commercial accelerators. Plug and Play is a large accelerator, based in Sunnyvale. It houses about 400 startups and offers three-month business development programs. Plug and Play is a general accelerator but focuses on several 'verticals' (i.e. targeting a specific industry, trade or customer type) such as financial technology, retail, health & wellness, new materials, mobility, food, insurance, the Internet of things, supply chain & logistics, sustainability, and travel and hospitality. Saeed Amidi, Plug and Play's founder and CEO, had a clear vision when he started his accelerator: "It is an investment vehicle. I get a chance to meet all these startups and I may have a chance to invest there. The next Google, the next PayPal, the next big thing. Our primary goal is to invest in promising startups. I would say that is 90% of our focus." Saeed truly believes in the power and impact of technology: "I feel that innovation and disruption are going to radically change the industrial world, the corporate world, banking, insurance, automobile industry, the retail industry, etc."

500 Startups, another large commercial accelerator, strives for fast startup growth through its four-month seed programs. Partner Elizabeth Yin explains: "We're trying to scale venture capital. This is something that I don't think anybody has done before. A traditional VC might invest in maybe ten companies a year and the firm is relatively small. We're investing in hundreds of startups around the globe on all six continents, and we have over a hundred people who work here at 500 Startups. Our focus is growth acceleration of startups in a slightly later seed stage. We're teaching them about how to optimize their customer acquisition and how to raise funds." 500 Startups is a general accelerator as well, taking on startups in areas ranging from consumer commerce to food technology, from cloud services to education, from financial technology to the Internet of things/drones/hardware.

The Alchemist Accelerator (San Francisco) is centered on growing startups that earn their revenues from enterprises rather than consumers – both business to business (B2B) and business to business to consumer (B2B2C). COO and partner Danielle D'Agostaro explains: "We built Alchemist around accelerating the sales process and the fundraising process because that's what it's going to take in order to get an enterprise company to scale." The Alchemist is deliberately sector-agnostic. As Danielle clarifies: "Because we are so broad in enterprise, we get startups that are building technologies in all realms, including space, quantum computers, rockets, human genome. Along with the software and the hardware and drones and computer vision, the possibilities are really endless, and we find that actually really exciting because we get a wide breadth of founders that come through here."

Naomi Kokubo of Founders Space (San Francisco) needs just a few words to summarize her accelerator's unique selling point: "The international scope and the strong educational focus." She continues: "A lot of accelerators wait for startups to come to Silicon Valley because the Valley is a magnet, people come from everywhere. We have a different philosophy, we partner with governments, universities, tech centers and other organizations in China, Korea, Taiwan, Europe, and they like to send their startups over here."

TiE LaunchPad, a general B2B accelerator based in Sunnyvale, is linked to TiE, which is a well-known mentoring and networking organization in Silicon Valley. In its earlier years, the primary focus of TiE was on empowering Southeast Asian immigrants to help them launch businesses of their own. Prashant Shah elucidates: "To support people from India, Bangladesh, Pakistan to help them become better entrepreneurs, to become accepted Silicon Valley entrepreneurs. It started as a mentorship driven kind of organization, non-profit, and the model just exploded." Given the great number of Asian entrepreneurs and companies in the Valley, it definitely appears that TiE's mission has succeeded. As Prashant proudly concludes: "It has been a phenomenal success." Now, membership in TiE's accelerator program is more open, and it no longer focuses exclusively on Southeast Asian founders. TiE LaunchPad started in 2014 as an accelerator within TiE as a way to formalize funding, mentoring, and workshops in a format that today's entrepreneurs are familiar with. I asked Prashant what the secret of LaunchPad's accelerator formula is: "We provide this deep mentorship, deep access into the entire ecosystem, deep access to all of these executives in our organization and have them help us help these companies. The cornerstone of our philosophy is that entrepreneurship is a great way of actually creating wealth."

HAX is a San Francisco hardware accelerator. Cyril Ebersweiler, the founder and managing director of HAX, has an interesting perspective. He does not applaud the Silicon Valley mantra on failure – on the contrary: "For me, an accelerator is the exact opposite. Nine out of ten startups should succeed. Why would you build something that just doesn't get you to market? At HAX, the goal is to get a hundred percent of the products go to market and we have 200 startups. We have reduced the part of shipping failure to close to nothing. We are well on our way to revolutionizing venture capital." HAX is focused on the consumer hardware space, but also B2B and robotics.

BootUP (Menlo Park) developed an almost holistic vision on what a good accelerator should be. As co-founder and partner Marco Ten Vaanholt explains: "We started BootUP to create a micro-ecosystem around entrepreneurialism. We believe that entrepreneurialism transcends race, religion, color of skin, and is the only way to avoid wars and to create prosperity. Our intent is to create a repeatable ecosystem that we can apply not only in Silicon Valley but also abroad. The idea is to elevate entrepreneurialism as a whole and that's why we started it." BootUP is a commercial venture, but its mission goes deeper than that. As Marco points out: "All of the partners in BootUP have done favorably well, they are well off, and we feel it is time to give back; that is one of the basic drivers. Our time to give back is really about trying to elevate our learning and help startups and scale-ups to go to the next stage." BootUP attracts startups from various sectors but tends to focus on new energy software, new generation aerospace big data, medical technology, and next-generation communications. As will be shown in the next chapter, BootUP creates its micro-ecosystem through a variety of services which are all about "reducing the risk of failure and improving the success rates of startups. That's the core philosophy at BootUP."

Samsung NEXT Start – which was previously called the Samsung Accelerator – invests in seed-stage startups and entrepreneurs-in-residence. It offers co-located spaces with funding, expertise, mentoring, and access to a growing alumni community. It is most similar to a corporate accelerator but has multiple models available to support founders and startups in achieving the perfect product-market fit. NEXT Start has offices in San Francisco, New York, and Tel Aviv. It is looking for software startups that develop innovative technologies in the field of augmented reality/virtual reality, the Internet of things, mobility (connected car, drones), data and analytics, machine learning and artificial intelligence, mobile health, payments, and smart cities. And NEXT Start is all about scaling and driving entrepreneurial excellence. As Gary Coover emphasizes: "We really focus on recruiting experienced founders and bringing them the best resources Samsung has to offer. We bring them unparalleled access to the ecosystem and the assets that help them scale and help them achieve their goals." In many cases, this is measured by helping a seed-stage startup get into a series A and beyond. Gary adds: "We also have an in-residence program where we will internally incubate startups either acquired by a Samsung business unit or spun out."

What about the core philosophy of the two university-linked accelerators, StartX and the Babson College Accelerator? StartX (Palo Alto) began as an initiative of Stanford students and recent alumni to create a central place on Stanford campus where starting entrepreneurs could get quick and trusted advice with respect to all sorts of new business challenges – where people in the Stanford ecosystem – students, faculty, alumni – could turn to in trying to scale their business, find product-market fit, raise money. A place where they could go for help," as Brian Hoffman puts it. Brian explains that StartX is all about pooling people and matchmaking between Stanford startup entrepreneurs and Stanford experts and mentors. "Our philosophy is to collect the best people from the Stanford ecosystem and bring them in, identify who is very good at what, and match them with our startup founder teams."

The Babson College accelerator focuses on supporting students and alumni to build, launch, and grow their business. It is based on a long tradition, as Babson is one of the best U.S. colleges teaching entrepreneurship and has been so for many years. Says Cindy Klein-Marmer: "Most students come to Babson because of an interest in entrepreneurship. A lot of students start a small business. Our main goal is to help them scale. Our program is on traction, on sales and marketing, on spirit and passion." The Babson accelerator targets both technology and industry indifferent startups can be both high-tech and low-tech.

The smaller, for-profit specialized accelerators have a different investment logic. They focus on coaching a (very) limited number of promising startups and bringing them to market. Usually the focus is on domain-specific technologies, and mentor programs tend to be very intense and hands on. They generally do not work with cohorts or batches. The Hive, the Palo Alto-based co-creation studio, is a good example. T.M. Ravi, The Hive's co-founder and managing director, frames mainstream general large-scale accelerators as follows: "They tend to be high-volume, they have classes of large numbers of startups, they tend to put in small amounts of money in these companies, they give them space, they give them tools, teach them entrepreneurship, and they are out in a few months. They are best suited for budding entrepreneurs in the consumer space." Ravi had a different concept for his accelerator: "The Hive is a venture studio which is low-volume; we do four to five startups a year. We're high-touch, we are very, very actively operationally involved with our companies. The Hive works with these companies to bring them to the next stage, not just by giving them money, but helping them fine-tune their business idea, helping put the team together, building early customers and partners, and getting them to the next round of financing, which is typically a series A round." The Hive's startups focus on specific technologies that are for the most part AI, context computing, autonomous agents, ambient intelligence, blockchain, enterprise, IoT, security, and financial services.

The Fabric (Mountain View), is another example of a specialized/high-touch accelerator approach. Its particular interest is in infrastructure and networking technologies. According to Prem Talreja: "We're not creating the next Airbnb, we're not creating the next Facebook, we are helping create companies that will transform the data center infrastructure. (...) We help six or seven companies flourish under our thinking; that's really what The Fabric is about. We don't just fund companies, we collaborate with entrepreneurs to co-create them."

Tandem, a smaller, for-profit accelerator, located in Burlingame, was founded by a couple of successful former entrepreneurs who get satisfaction out of coaching and investing in startups. Managing partner Sunil Bhargava recounts the story of how Tandem started. "I'd done a couple of startups, I just sold my last company and I was kind of wondering what to do. I didn't really want to found another startup, because of family reasons, my kids were still young. So, initially I thought I'll take a year or two off and just be an angel investor and advisor. I tried that for three or four months and I found that it wasn't very gratifying. I think when you don't have enough time or money in a startup, you tend to treat it as a part-time job and you are not really understanding the early chaotic stages of a new venture. I wanted to be more deeply involved in startups but I didn't want to be a founder." Tandem focuses on mobile applications. Sunil puts Tandem's strength down to the following: "We basically work with our companies and we enjoy that process. We help them with the most important thing: getting traction. Each Tandem partner becomes a champion of the startups we coach. We mutually inject each other with our enthusiasm."

These three smaller, for-profit accelerators have in common that they focus on specific technological domains (artificial intelligence, mobile, cloud infrastructure), whereas the core philosophy of the next four smaller accelerators I will discuss focuses on particular target groups and problem areas. I refer to these two groups of low-volume/high-touch accelerators as domain-specific accelerators and niche accelerators, respectively.

Women's Startup Lab (Menlo Park) is a niche accelerator with a very outspoken mission: to empower female founders and to create strong startups that make a difference in the world. As founder and CEO Ari Horie states: "Our bigger goal is to make the world a better place with women leaders influencing through technology advancement. We need female leaders to shape the world. There is so much need for women to be part of technology growth and opportunities, to make a positive impact by driving a scalable, ethical, and sustainable business world. Not having women participating is like reaching our business potential only halfway." Women's Startup Lab has an interesting philosophy: "We focus on the entire founder's growth and collaborative mindset, what we call 'hitology'. It's about the founder, the founder's performance, and the startup's growth through community and collaboration. Our program is very person-centered." She defines hitology – derived from the Japanese concept of 'hito' (meaning 'human') – as people supporting and holding each other accountable for extraordinary results. Women's Startup Lab is not only about accelerating the startup's core business but also about transforming the startup's founder herself.

Powerhouse is an Oakland-based niche accelerator that aims to grow solar energy startups and help them to go to market. Co-founder and CEO Emily Kirsch has a clear Silicon-Valley-style vision for Powerhouse: "Our philosophy is that solar will become the most abundant and affordable resource in the world in our lifetime. Our mission is to make solar the go-to energy source for everyone in the world." Big thinking, that's for sure. Powerhouse is mission-driven "but for-profit," as Emily adds.

Imagine H_2O, San Francisco, another niche accelerator, is mission-driven too but non-profit. Its objective is to turn water challenges into opportunities and to offer promising water entrepreneurs and startups a path to market and an opportunity to scale their businesses. Its USP is that it operates as a virtual network accelerator with online remote mentoring as well as some physical interaction. Tom Ferguson, vice president of programming, explains to me that "network is everything in the water industry, and we have the networks. We have a solid understanding of the vagaries of the industry itself, we know the stakeholders and they know us."

Cleantech Open is a non-profit niche accelerator focused on growing early-stage startup companies that offer solutions to environmental and energy problems. Its ambitious mission, as executive director Ian Foraker puts it is: "To find, fund, and foster the most promising cleantech startups on the planet." Cleantech Open operates globally; in the U.S. it works with a mentor and support force of over 2,000 volunteers who implement the coaching program. Ian defines its unique selling point as follows: "We have a very clear focus: clean technology. We have a community that we have built over ten years, a lot of great people are in our network. We have a very robust network, connected with leading organizations, and leading social professions."

Accelerator platforms are slightly different from accelerators in that they are platforms that help startups to grow by offering co-working space and a community of practice and peers. In this study, I interviewed people at five accelerator platforms: Runway, GSVlabs, Prospect Silicon Valley, Hacker Dojo, and RocketSpace.

Runway is a co-working space and accelerator for high-growth startups that is housed in the San Francisco Twitter building. Its primary goal and philosophy according to former managing director Matt Walters is as follows: "We want to create a community of startups, we want them to collaborate, we want to engage with them. When it's done authentically it creates great results." Starting a new business is natural to this generation of young people, Matt observes: "Especially here in Silicon Valley it's almost peer pressure, like 'if you are not starting a company, what is wrong with you?'".

GSVlabs is a co-working space based in Redwood City. CEO Marlon Evans explains its unique selling point as follows: "Our niche is focusing on seed to series A companies. The majority of our companies can stay here for 12 months, they can stay for 18 months. It's not cyclical. And we have real focus on subject matter expertise across our verticals. We look at mobile, big data, education technology, sustainability, and entertainment."

Prospect Silicon Valley, San Jose, describes itself as a non-profit demonstration center and innovation hub specialized in promoting the adoption of practical solutions to mobility, transportation, energy, and the built environment. Founder and former CEO Doug Davenport describes what differentiates Prospect Silicon Valley from other accelerators: "Our unique approach is in assisting startups that are trying to solve a practical problem to link with the stakeholders in that very problem area, both in the public sector and corporate agencies." This stakeholder approach is interesting because it creates a distinct focus. As Doug explains: "We are focused on markets where the customer is a cloud of various interests, relationships, roles that are being played by various stakeholders. We navigate out startups through this stakeholder system and partner network so they can give them their first real demonstration which can possibly give them their first customer."

Hacker Dojo did not start as the co-working space it is has become; it was much more loosely and informally "organized". As executive director Jun Wong clarifies: "It was really just a place where like-minded people, mostly software developers working at various companies in Silicon Valley met together after work. Over time, makers, hardware enthusiasts, and startups discovered they could hack the system and use us as the most affordable co-working space in the Valley." In 2016, Hacker Dojo moved to its present location in Santa Clara where it rents a 16,600 square-foot community center and hacker space. It is non-profit and wants to stays that way: "Silicon Valley becomes more and more expensive to live. The ability to incubate things becomes quite expensive and so Hacker Dojo does provide one of the only places where you can have workspace at a really affordable price. We want to be as affordable as possible to the public." Jun's point of view is quite uncommon in an area where money rules and where the cost of living is one of the highest in the world.

RocketSpace is a large and well-known co-working campus in San Francisco. Duncan Logan, the founder and CEO, articulates what makes RocketSpace special: "I think the difference at RocketSpace is that everyone here is so deadly serious about building a billion-dollar company. We want to create a really brilliant environment for entrepreneurs to succeed. We're kind of co-working on steroids." Duncan developed a 'disruptive' philosophy on letting startups into RocketSpace: "It was one of the first co-working spaces that had a selection process. And the harder we selected, so the more exclusive we became, the more people wanted to be here."

The analysis above clearly shows the main differences between accelerators in how they define their core philosophy, their focus, and their unique selling points. A main taxonomic difference is whether accelerators are technology-agnostic – i.e., not focused on a particular technological domain – or concentrate on tracing high potentials in specific technological domains. But even the larger, more general accelerators use some segmentation format, for example by introducing verticals. The smaller accelerators typically focus on particular markets corresponding to specific technological or societal problems. These smaller, domain-specific accelerators and niche accelerators are the ones in which executive team members significantly invest in hands-on coaching of admitted startups, personally working with them to bring them to the next level.

Business model

Accelerators differ in their business purpose, the venture achievements they seek, their scaling philosophy, and their investment goals. Most accelerators are for-profit, but some are non-profit, mission-driven organizations. But they all share the determination to scale and grow startups and bring them to an advanced stage. In this section, I examine the various business models Silicon Valley accelerators are based on, particularly regarding their investment strategy, equity policy, and startup numbers, in order to provide insight into the way these accelerators operate from a business point of view. How much do they invest in the startups they admit? Do they take equity, and if so, how much? Are they backed by a venture fund? What are the business metrics they look for? The statistics that will be mentioned are from the executive interviews and from the accelerators' websites.

500 Startups is one of the largest general accelerators in Silicon Valley and is based in Mountain View and San Francisco. It has invested in over 1,800 startups and more than 3,000 founders from over 60 countries. It manages over $250 million in assets. How much does 500 Startups invest in its companies? Partner Elizabeth Yin: "Technically, we invest $150,000 in each accelerated company but we do hold back $37,500 dollars for fees – to pay for the office, to pay for the coaches, to pay for mentorship, etc." Startup 500 offers the $150,000 gross investment for 6% equity.

Plug and Play's business model is also based on high volume. It is probably the world's largest accelerator with over 20 locations worldwide. Plug and Play has accelerated more than 2,000 startups since 2006, from pre-product to series A. Investments range from $25,000 to $500,000; equity varies but is typically about 5%. It claims that its startup companies combined have raised over $5 billion in additional funding. Plug and Play is all about return on investment, about picking winners at an early stage. CEO Saeed Amidi: "Last year I invested in 160 companies. Our business model is to invest in startups like Dropbox when it was only two people, Lending Club when it was two people." Both post-unicorn startups became tremendously successful companies. These are the kinds of investment darlings that Plug and Play is looking for.

The Alchemist Accelerator is dedicated to enterprise startups and seeds about 40-50 new ventures per year. It is backed by investors such as Cisco, Draper Fisher Jurvetson, Foundation Capital, Khosla Ventures, Siemens, and Salesforce.com. Since late 2014, 30 of its companies have raised on average $2 million, and 12 of its companies have been acquired. Danielle D'Agostaro explains the Alchemist's investment policy: "We give about $60K to our startups from which they pay a tuition of around $24K. So they are left with about $36K and we take around 5% equity, but that is negotiable. It's really not meant as an investment vehicle, we just want to make sure we are taking each other seriously. The investors' fund does not pay out our organization fee, so this way Alchemist is able to sustain itself." Danielle emphasizes that the Alchemist backers are not primarily involved for ROI. "They are not looking to get their money back, they are looking at it from a strategic point of view. What are the new technologies that are going to help keep them special in the future? Through our accelerator they have an opportunity to tap into those companies."

Founders Space invests in seed and early-stage ventures and has partners in over twenty countries with a strong presence in Asia. It offers an online incubator program as well as live classes in its accelerator program. The business model is based on tuition fees and on equity. Naomi Kokubo: "Equity ranges between 0.5% and 5%; it depends on the startup team. We don't guarantee investment but we do ask every startup who joins our program to give us participation rights for future investment rounds." Corporate programs, Naomi adds, are based on individual contracts.

TiE LaunchPad is a smaller accelerator for enterprise startups that takes five to eight companies per batch. It is backed by a TiE charter member VC fund of about $5 million. LaunchPad provides a $50,000 investment in convertible notes and charges a 4% equity fee. Accepted startups are asked to allow TiE charter members to invest up to 10% of the next funding round. Dedicated startup team mentors receive 0.25% of the equity fee. Prashant Shah of TiE LaunchPad, finds that this formula works well. "The fact that we have a fund gives us a fiduciary responsibility. We have to try to return money for our investors as well, so we have to be careful about where we invest. We want to invest in good founders, good companies. We know it is going to take a while before they get to some kind of exit and we are up for that challenge. We know it takes time."

Hardware accelerator HAX in San Francisco focuses on finalizing startup prototypes; teams need to relocate to HAX's office in Shenzhen, China for about four months. Shenzhen is called the 'Silicon Valley of Hardware' or even the 'World Capital of Hardware'.[67] HAX does not charge fees but offers seed capital: $25,000 for 6% equity, $100,000 for 9% equity (6% common stock, a credit-linked note (CLN) which converts to 3% equity at the next financing round in exchange for participation), and up to $200,000 extra in matching funds. HAX is backed by SOSV, an investment company that has funded over 500 startups (150 per year) with seed, venture, and growth-stage funding. SOSV has $250 million in assets under management. Cyril Ebersweiler, partner at SOSV and managing director of HAX, clarifies the business model: "We call ourselves 'the accelerator VC'. We will exit when our startup companies exit, that is the only agenda here. That is the only thing that is going on." Running an accelerator is like running a startup, according to Cyril: "Accelerators are extremely time consuming, resource consuming, exhausting. What people don't understand is that people running accelerators are entrepreneurs. It is a startup." Recently, SOSV founded two new accelerators: Food HAX in New York City and the synthetic biology accelerator IndieBio in San Francisco.

BootUP is a miniature ecosystem aiming to grow startups. It rents co-working office space, provides mentorship, invests in high-potential startups, and gives access to high-caliber network facilities. It has invested in over 120 startups that have raised over $400 million and have an overall valuation of $4 billion. The office space business model is straightforward: rent. As Marco ten Vaanholt states: "Space is just a box. We look at the business idea and if it's complementary to any of the other startups in our building. But there's just rent to be paid." BootUP's investment policy is based on revenue sharing or equity. It depends on the team and the company. "Smart entrepreneurs don't like to give up equity but are willing to give revenue share. That's the starting of a relationship. We often work on master-based revenue share if we can get a deal from them. That's how we get a portion of the pie." BootUP does a lot of matchmaking between corporates and startups. "And only then we take equity." Marco's investment math is simple: selectivity. "I would rather have 25 startups of which 15 or 20 do well, than 100 of which five do well. That's really the difference between a standard accelerator or incubator and what we try to do here at BootUP." How much equity do Marco and his partners take? "It depends on the stage of the company. If it's an earlier stage company we take between five and ten percent. If it's a later-stage company it can be between two and five percent. It depends on what the value of the company is as well as how much work we are going to do as a team."

Samsung NEXT Start, the corporate accelerator, focuses on experienced entrepreneurs and offers two models: a seed funding model and an in-residence model. In the first model, startup teams are provided with stage-specific resources and expertise "to go from seed to series A and beyond". The second model is a program "where we internally incubate companies that when successful are either acquired by Samsung or spun out" (Gary Coover). The seed funding model offers funding of between $100,000 and $1 million, co-location for three-plus months, and a host of other resources like access to alumni and mentor networks. The in-residence program has a longer runway due to the involvement of Samsung – anywhere from three to 18 months.

Now let's take a look at the business models of the two university and college-linked accelerators. StartX, the Stanford-University-affiliated accelerator, is all about activating the notorious Stanford ecosystem in order to allow new ventures and innovative business ideas to grow faster. As executive Brian Hoffman says: "StartX is about bringing the best Stanford people together and making them more successful faster. We don't take equity, we are structured as a non-profit, because the very best people we want in our community are not going to join an accelerator where they have to give up a sizeable amount of their company for a small seed check." StartX has 12,600 square feet of office space, 2,000 of which is lab space, which it rents to startup companies. Brian also emphasizes that the real value of StartX is the Stanford community network. "That's what people are coming for, not for office space." StartX gets its money from corporate sponsorships (such as Microsoft, Panasonics, Johnson & Johnson, Ford), who want early and preferential access to talent and technology. These partnerships are based on the corporate understanding that "to stay competitive, they need access to early-stage innovations." The larger tiered corporate partnerships may involve contributions of between $100,000 and $200,000 a year. StartX, Stanford University, and Stanford Health Care have a joint investment fund (SSF) since 2013, which has invested over $100 million in 200+ StartX companies, available only to Stanford-affiliated founders.

The Babson College venture accelerator program centers on students and Babson alumni. According to Cindy Klein-Marmer: "We support them in many ways. We pay for their housing, on-campus housing if they select to live on campus. We provide them with meals throughout the program summer period. We provide them with workshops or what we call 'lunch and learning sessions'." The accelerator program works with limited overhead. "We run very lean: just two staffers that run it on a daily basis, and we have one or two interns. Faculty is paid in an equivalent of course exemptions. So it will count as part of their class, and not separate from the program. Moreover, it gives them exposure to the corporate world." Cindy underlines the two-way process of faculty involvement: it gives them access to early-stage entrepreneurship, and they can use these practical examples in their teaching. When asked whether Babson offers funding to its student ventures, Cindy responds: "We do have a seed funding opportunity. We give money through which I like to think of as a 'prototyping fund'. It's smaller dollars, anywhere from a few hundred dollars to a few thousand dollars. Our cap right now is five thousand dollars. We are not an ATM machine, but if you are awarded it, you are not expected to have to pay it back."

The Hive is a smaller, high-touch, for-profit, domain-specific venture studio that takes in about five startups a year but on a very intensive coaching basis. The Hive provides smart money and cash investments. As T.M. Ravi clarifies: "We typically invest between $2 million to $3 million in our startups. That's significant money for such an early-stage company. But we work with our companies, help them fine-tune the business idea, help them put their team together, and develop the product. We do so for 12 to 15 months. We get joined at the hip with our startup founders." The Hive's investment goals go hand in hand with its high-touch involvement with its startups. "We are very hands-on with the company till it gets to the next round of finance, which is usually a series A round and they would generally raise anywhere from $10 million to $20 million." And what happens after this round? "Much like the other VCs, we will be a part of the company's board, provide high-level guidance, insight, and introductions but not day-to-day operation." Does The Hive take equity? If the company is based on a business idea developed by The Hive, then The Hive becomes a co-founder. If the company is already founded, then The Hive receives equity for its investment. As T.M. Ravi spells out: "This equity is at a very early stage where the risk of failure is high. We come in at a high-risk stage and with the hands-on guidance of our team, as well as the capital we provide, we're putting them on the path to success."

The Fabric is a similar co-creation new venture accelerator. It works with only one or two startup companies at any time. The Fabric actively works with the founder entrepreneurs to refine their idea and then provides seeds financing of $1 million to $1.5 million per company. The investment goal is to prepare the startups for high-quality series A funding by providing them with a viable business model, a prototype, market validation, and by developing the team. The Fabric is backed by an investment fund of roughly $10 million, and investors own equity in The Fabric. It is clearly a for-profit model, as Prem Talreja emphasizes: "We are doing it for the return on investment, we are doing it for the responsibility we have toward our shareholders." But The Fabric team members, all seasoned entrepreneurs, are also personally motivated to create successes, as is clear from the way Prem frames his motivation: "What is exciting for me is that I'm still able to give back. I'm still relevant to the industry that created me, the industry that has given me so much. After all, this is Silicon Valley."

Tandem is another smaller, for-profit, domain-specific accelerator that seeds hardware and software mobile startups. It is now a $100 million investment fund that puts in an initial investment of $200,000 to $2 million and substantial follow-on investing. Tandem is a co-creation studio accelerator that does two types of investments. Sunil Bhargava explains: "We do traditional seed investments, like an investor. We put in less time. But a proportion of our deals during the early phase of a new fund is where we use our studio, where we are actively involved with growing startup companies over a 6-12 month period. Help them to build their company and help them getting traction. We call this active or early seed." I ask Sunil whether Tandem takes equity: "Sure. We take equity for the money we put in. In the six-month active seed deals, we take up to 10% common equity. We do not take common equity in the later-stage seed deals." Tandem has scaled up its acceleration program since it started in 2007: it has moved from doing 10 startups a year to 20 startups over two years, to 80 startups over four years.

What about the business economics of the four niche accelerators that are part of my sample? Powerhouse and Women's Startup Lab are two smaller, specialized, high-touch accelerators, about solar energy and empowering women entrepreneurs, respectively. What do their business models look like? Powerhouse offers $10,000 cash investments to startup companies in its six-month accelerator program as well as free office space, non-dilutive grant opportunities, and the right to invest up to $50,000 in exchange for a convertible note and warrant. Powerhouse takes up to 5% equity in its startups. Emily Kirsch underlines that her for-profit business model has a clear purpose: "We think that by having a business model that is dependent on success or failure of our companies, we will have better rates of success with our startups. We don't continue to survive unless our companies do well." Powerhouse also has an incubator which is based on a monthly recurring revenue model, and it does sponsored events. The $10,000 initial cash investment is "just to show some skin in the game. To give them a jump start into their fundraising process. Our role is to help them raise capital for the next seed round."

Women's Startup Lab is a founder development niche accelerator based in Menlo Park. The program's fee is $10,000, but as founder Ari Horie self-consciously adds: "It's $85,000 worth of content." If Women's Startup Lab invests in startups, it takes about 6% equity. Ari emphasizes that her revenue model differs radically from standard VC business models: "We care about the education part of our program, we are founder-centric, we offer a holistic approach, we do founder development." The educational program at Women's Startup Lab for startup founders as well as its sponsorships and corporate entrepreneur programs generate enough revenue to sustain its operation.

Imagine H_2O and Cleantech Open, located in San Francisco and Redwood City respectively, are two non-profit, mission-driven, niche accelerators that focus on strengthening startups marketing practical solutions to environmental problems. Tom Ferguson explains Imagine H_2O's funding model, which is definitely not about taking equity in startup companies. Its business model is based on remote support through its virtual accelerator. "We keep our overheads low. It allows us not to be the kind of accelerator that says: 'We take five percent of your business for $20K'. To me that is an uncomfortable proposition, especially if you require them to relocate for a certain amount of time." Tom continues: "If you were to really be serious about looking through the lens of the startups, something like $175,000 is a different thing. You can hire two excellent people with options for one year that get you further down the road. That, I think, is worth giving up that portion of your company." Director Nimesh Modak explains that Imagine H_2O is entirely grant supported (Wells Fargo is the head sponsor) and is also involved in some consultancy work. This allows the accelerator program itself to be free of costs for admitted participants, apart from a modest nominal application fee. Startups compete for a yearly total of $25,000 prize money for the best water problem solution idea. But as Tom says: "The real value of our program is in our network."

Cleantech Open is a volunteer organization providing support to startups that address sustainability issues. "Because of that", Ian Foraker points out, "we have a very low price point. We don't take equity, we just have an application fee of $150, and when companies are accepted into the program, it's a participation fee of $1,200. And that's all. We're able to deliver value without a huge overhead. Over 90% of our operations as an organization is pro bono." Cleantech's startup awards are funded by its corporate sponsors, and they organize showcasing events. Neither Cleantech Open nor Imagine H_2O offer in-house office space to their participating startup companies.

Harm TenHoff, CEO of BayLink, is very critical about the practice of taking equity in startups. He argues that: "Taking 5% or 8% equity for $50,000 to $100,000 is a lot of money for startups to give away. There is a downside to it. If you have been in an accelerator and don't get funded, you're sort of blacklisted. Nobody wants to touch you anymore. No serial or seasoned entrepreneur will go into such an accelerator because they don't want to give up that amount of equity."

Finally, I have a look at the business models that Silicon Valley platform accelerators work with that get their revenue from renting co-working space, from creating dynamic and entrepreneurial environments for startups to thrive and grow. GSVlabs is a large 72,000 square-foot campus in Redwood City that houses 170 startups and whose companies have raised over $250 million. It is backed by the GSV Financial Group, a merchant bank. Marlon Evans explains that companies pay a monthly fee per desk: "It's all included: your IT, your printing, your coffee, your mentorship, your events, your workshops." GSVlabs also gets revenues from sponsored events, corporate partnerships, accelerating programs for International clients.

Until recently, Matt Walters ran the 30,000-square-foot co-working space and startup hub Runway in downtown San Francisco. Runway is home to about 85 startups and 200 startup team founders. Matt explains that its main revenue is rent, "But the other thing we do is consulting for major corporations. They look for technology advice, for startups to partner with – in FinTech [financial technology], for instance. And we have corporate sponsorships and partnerships."

Hacker Dojo has a membership-based revenue model. It offers co-working space and maker space in its 16,000-square-foot non-profit community center and hackerlab. Its startup philosophy, as director Jun Wong tells me, is "to really offer inexpensive incubation time. We try to run at a low budget as possible so that we can still be as affordable as possible to those who need it." Hacker does not use the accelerator business model of investment and equity. "Once you start to offer such services, you have to rank your companies, right? We don't want that. We avoid ranking the people that are here. We want this to be a safe haven. Hacker Dojo provides a very unbiased and a very open space where people can work." Besides membership fees, Hacker receives donations from both individuals and organizations, and from high-tech corporates.

Prospect SV is an innovation hub and 23,000-square-foot demonstration center in San Jose with a focus on transportation, energy, and the physical environment. Prospect is a non-profit organization. Doug Davenport: "There are non-profit business accelerators that will take ownership stakes in their companies. We don't do that." Prospect's business philosophy is to focus on public sector problems in the built environment by aligning multiple stakeholders regarding practical commercial solutions. "Equity is not part of our income model because we want to be able to work with the public sector as an impartial solutions-oriented group. That reputation is very important to us." Prospect SV's funding mainly comes from corporate sponsors, a modest monthly fee from its startup clients, and from non-diluted government grants. It has helped 25+ startup clients with demonstration and scaling projects, and these startups have raised over $145 million in capital investment, attracted $50 million in community financing, and are collaborating with 50 city partners.

RocketSpace, to conclude the description and analysis of the accelerator business models, is a large co-working space and accelerator in San Francisco's financial district. It has hosted over 800 startups since 2011 and houses 200 startups on campus. Its business metrics include 16 unicorn alumni companies, 1.5 startups per week that secure funding, and an average total of $18 million in funds raised by its startup members. RocketSpace's revenues come from rent paid by startups, corporates from around the world, consultancy projects, and industry acceleration programs. "We probably have four or five executive teams from corporations here every week," says Duncan Logan. Some of RocketSpace's alumni have been extremely successful, including Uber, Spotify, and Supercell, which are now worth billions. When I ask Duncan whether he regrets that his co-working space and accelerator has a no-equity policy, his response is prescient: "Maybe analysts who look at RocketSpace in twenty years' time will conclude: 'If only they took equity, they'd be the best performing investment fund in the world.' But the truth is, if we took equity, we wouldn't attract the very best companies here in Silicon Valley – because, you know, the very best don't need to give equity."

As is clear from the above, Silicon Valley accelerators differ significantly in business model and revenue policy. The investment policy of general/low-touch, for-profit accelerators is to find early-stage startup diamonds. Their 'spray and pray' business strategy is all about spotting scalable startups with massive market potential, based on the belief that the few winners will make up for the many losses. For these reasons, they favor software startups. The smaller specialized/high-touch, for-profit accelerators have an investment policy in which accelerator executives work hands-on with just a few, carefully selected startup teams. Getting traction is the main focus, and teams are mentored by executives who are experienced entrepreneurs.

For-profit accelerators are typically backed by investment funds, often institutional investors. By contrast, non-profit accelerators' business models are usually based on (combinations of) participation fees, corporate donations, foundation grants, or consultancy projects. Rent, obviously, is a main source of revenue for co-working spaces. But all business models are inspired by finding ways to connect startup teams, mentors, stakeholders, and investors in order to successfully market new ventures.

External cooperation

There is growing interest within the academic literature and the literature on applied innovation in understanding how cooperation facilitates innovation or, more precisely, the way successful innovation trajectories are strengthened by effective business cooperation models (Bauwen 2013; Koster 2016; Barringer & Harrison 2000; Fjeldstad et al. 2012; Gal et al. 2014). As I outlined above, cooperation is a structural feature of the Silicon Valley innovation and startup ecosystem and has been so for many decades. It is an intrinsic characteristic of the Valley's entrepreneurial mindset.

How important is collaborating with external partners in the Valley's ecosystem for accelerator executives? When I ask The Hive's CEO T.M. Ravi whether cooperation is a high priority on his accelerators' network agenda, his reply is unequivocal: "Absolutely. We do three types of collaborations. One is with venture capitalists, because they are long-term capital partners for our companies. The second is with universities: faculty members at Stanford, Berkeley, Carnegie Melon, MIT. We explore to see if we can create companies out of their research. We bring in their summer students. And the third is with corporations. They are great as go-to-market partners and they have deep domain expertise."

Networking is elementary. Danielle D'Agostaro of Alchemist expounds: "We do a lot of external outreach. We talk at meetings with potential startups, have relations with international schools. We have created a very diverse network of people around the world, which makes our brand pretty strong. Our founder and managing director is a Stanford University business professor." Alchemist also has partnerships with service providers in cloud hosting and legal banking, and even arranges gym memberships for its participants.

Investors are indispensable partners for accelerators. Saeed Amidi of Plug and Play underlines this: "We review over 1,000 startups per industry and we choose 50 of them to pitch to us and to our partners. In our FinTech vertical, for example, we have 16 out of the top 20 banks in the world as our partner. We have the two biggest Japanese banks, we have Deutsche Bank, we have Santander, we have BNP Paribas, we have Credit Suisse. And we love universities. We have 50 great universities we work with, such as Stanford, MIT, Carnegie Mellon." Plug and Play also actively collaborates with universities: "We are very close to their engineering schools and business schools. We participate in their business plan competitions and their labs. A lot of innovation happens in university labs. And that's where we come in. We come in to seed fund their startups and to bring them additional funding and additional growth. Our main objective is to find great technology and great entrepreneurs. I would say at least 50% of our investments are first-time entrepreneurs straight out of the university." Plug and Play, moreover, has a very engaged international corporate program in which it partners with over 180 major corporations.

StartX in Palo Alto closely works with Stanford University and its faculty members, an obvious partnership given that StartX spun out of the Stanford Student Enterprise lab. Recently the relationship between

StartX and Stanford has become more formalized. StartX's Brian Hoffman elucidates: "Now we have two contracts: one with the university and one with Stanford Hospital. They contribute an annual grant to us for our operations; two-thirds from the university, one-third from the hospital. They also operate an investment vehicle with us and have board seats. So in some way we ourselves are a startup, with Stanford and the hospital as the series A investors and with the Stanford community as mentors and advisors."

Domain knowledge is important in the accelerator partnership models and external networks. Cleantech Open works with numerous individual energy and environmental experts, mostly as volunteers. But they also have more structural collaborations. Ian Foraker: "We work with climate change groups at Berkeley. We have a partnership with the United Nations. We are active in eight regions in the U.S. and in many countries across the globe. We have a close relationship with the U.S. Department of Energy and with the State of California through its California Clean Energy Fund. Moreover, we partner with MassCEC and NYSERDA in the Northeast and the Colorado Cleantech Industries Association. And we are involved in organizing the Cleantech Open Global Ideas Competition, taking place as part of the Global Entrepreneurship Week."

Prospect Silicon Valley, the non-profit urban-tech innovation hub, works with several corporates including Cisco, Ford, Microsoft, Hyundai, Hitachi, Bank of America, and Wells Fargo. Doug Davenport remarks: "I find they all share a fascination with the future of the market. They like the idea that we are bringing people together. They like that they get to see things that are way beyond what their current offerings can provide. I found that some of them are very easy to convince because they see the value immediately, they see how this is aligned, see how they can take advantage of what we have." Sponsors get various things in return, according to Doug. "Our standard offer of corporate underwriting includes logo inclusions and other ways of recognition. We do preferential things like blog posts and publications. We do events that sponsors get to speak at. We connect them with other cities and we do engagement side work." Prospect also works with San Jose State University and won a grant with the Berkeley transportation sustainability center for advanced transportation technology. In addition, it makes part of its space available for its students to work on innovation projects.

GSVlabs partners with Google. CEO Marlon Evans describes it as: "A great partnership. They are bringing in all their mentors and executives to work with our startups." GSVlabs also partners with law firms and HR companies to assist their new businesses, "But what we don't want is that the companies are just selling into our community, so we structure where they come in. They will provide a seminar on hiring your first fifteen employees, or something like that. We invite our community to participate and the company might then host office hours for companies to go into a little bit more." GSVlabs sees the value of strategic partnerships with universities. Marlon: "My ultimate goal is to have a couple of universities that are based here in the Valley that are sending us students and be interns for our startups. These students could be a main resource who in turn get a firsthand experience of what it is like to work in a startup."

The Fabric focuses on corporates rather than on universities. Prem Talreja explains: "For us, the university is Cisco, VMware, HP, and other leaders because that's where the people are that value the problems and challenges we are working on. And for acquisition and partnership as well. These leaders like us because they might acquire one of our startups; they like to keep an eye on what we are doing."

What about a corporate accelerator such as Samsung NEXT? Do they work with outside partners? Gary Coover: "Sure, but nothing that we have formalized. We have quite a few relationships with other accelerators, investors, and universities that we will sometimes co-host events with and share pipeline. The broader Samsung NEXT organization also provides investment, partnership and acquisition opportunities for the startup community, which helps generate strong relationships with the VC community."

The Silicon Valley support system is widely used by my sample of accelerators, for example with respect to legal and HR facilitators. Imagine H_2O is a good example. Tom Ferguson notes that: "We have a fantastic legal partner who has supported the last two cohort intakes. It's all about relationships, also with their other clients. That's a really interesting secondary network effect." Emily Kirsch of Powerhouse shares this view: "The legal side is essential. We built a relationship with DLA Piper, one of the most famous law firms in the world. They have been absolutely incredible. They did a ton of work with our first cohort on a pro bono basis and were willing to take the early risk lawyers are not known for." Being connected to the venture community is fundamental as well: individual angel investors, small and large venture funds, and family businesses are important in this respect. Having solid external networks in the energy field is crucial for Powerhouse in regards of its technology focus. As Emily states: "Those partnerships are indispensable. We first and foremost have relationships with the solar incumbents as we call them – even so, many of them are less than 15 years old. SolarCity [a Silicon-Valley-based full-service solar provider] is one of our main partners and so are the thousands of small solar installers across the country. That's who our startups are serving."

Runway partners with Fenwick & West, which Matt Walters describes as: "One of the biggest law firms in Silicon Valley. They meet with our startups teams, e.g. with respect to IP issues. We are partnering with IBM, with AT&T, and with stakeholders in the EdTech field. We are talking to the CITRUS Invention Lab of Berkeley and we work with the University of San Francisco. But universities is one of the areas I think we could do a better job. It's a great talent pool." Samsung NEXT aims to provide its startups with options for resources. Gary Coover highlights a few of these options: "Amazon Web Services has an agreement with us to provide all of our teams with $100,000 free credits for the first year. We negotiate deals like that and provide preferred vendors and resources for them to access. The biggest value added is probably the recruiter we have on staff who is helping the startup teams hire engineers. One of the top problems for every startup is identifying and attracting great technical talent."

Lawyers play a valued role in the Silicon Valley world of accelerators. As Tandem's founder Sunil Bhargava expounds: "Lawyers are generally very good here in the Valley. We have a handful of those lawyers who we recommend to our startups, and they can choose whoever they want. We also have a number of lawyers that they can consult if they just need a one-on-one. Finding a good lawyer is not a problem." Founders Space also brings in lawyers regularly, as Naomi Kokubo explains: "We have lots of lawyers come; they give mentorship sessions on different issues such as IP, International Corporate Transaction, licensing issues, cap tables, etc. They don't charge any fees immediately but the startup teams may become future clients. Lawyers are also willing to forego payment until startups are funded." This is another example of the deferred fee system that is part of the Silicon Valley startup support structure helping new ventures in their early stage of development when revenues are minimal. This is also a stage in which startups are most in need of professional legal counsel and business advice. The deferred payment practice generally works fine and is seen as a smart solution to an otherwise difficult financial issue.

There is general agreement among the accelerator executives I interviewed about the strength and value of the support structure of Silicon Valley's ecosystem. Cooperation is and has been an elementary feature of this ecosystem for a long time. Linkages are informal but its goal and execution are highly institutionalized. Cooperation is an intrinsic part of Silicon Valley as a networking society and its culture of collaborating and sharing

Conclusion

In this chapter, I analyzed the differences between accelerators in terms of their startup growth paradigm and domain focus, business model, and cooperation strategy. The distinction between general/low-touch accelerators and specialized/high-touch accelerators turned out to be instrumental. The first type of accelerator is based on investment metrics that bring in several batches of startups per year in their permanent search for startups that combine rapid scalability and potentially large markets. Investing in such high potentials is the main investment strategy of these accelerators. Their ROI is founded on future traction and market penetration. The second type of accelerator does not take a cohort approach but helps to grow a limited number of startups in targeted technological or social domains and does so in a very intensive way. They are domain-specific or niche players. Their de-risking strategy is based on day-to-day coaching by highly experienced serial entrepreneurs. A successful exit is what they opt for.

The analysis also revealed that the distinction between incubators and accelerators is instrumental rather than conceptual. This conclusion was confirmed in a recent study by the California Business Incubation Alliance: "The proliferation of [incubator and accelerator] programs has blurred the traditional lines between these two types of support for entrepreneurs." (2016: 7).

Most Silicon Valley accelerators are for-profit businesses. Their goal is to invest in promising startups with scalability potential in return for equity or other forms of financial participation. These might be larger general or smaller specialized accelerators. Corporate accelerators may have seed investment funds, but their main purpose is to stay on par with major technological innovations that keep them competitive. Accelerators help corporates to track innovative startups. As Aiaz Kazi, who heads Google's Platform Ecosystem, points out: "I always say that startups are the lifeblood of innovation. Let them bubble up from the ground, give them a structure, give them a way that allows them to come through, and they will imagine and build solutions on your platform that you simply can't." But there is also another incentive, as Aiaz explains: "Some of these startups will grow and become big customers of tomorrow. You can bring startups into the mix to add on to your product, and that's a win for both."

Commercial co-working spaces are based on a rent business model but also provide access to their network of investors. The mission-driven, non-profit accelerators want their startups to grow because of their potential solutions to pressing social issues such as fighting climate change and water problems or promoting the adoption of clean technology innovations. Their revenues come from foundation grants, corporate sponsorships, government support, and consultancy. These accelerators may not themselves invest in their startup companies, but they often do have structured relationships with investors.

Have accelerators achieved success in launching viable startups? Accelerators like to brag about the funds raised by their startup alumni in later investment stages, which may easily run into the hundreds of millions and sometimes even billions of dollars. Their websites proudly present these funding figures. But the performance math is a bit more complicated then these statistics suggest. It is unclear whether there is a causal relationship between accelerator program participation and startup success. Startup performance is a complex phenomenon and depends on many factors, of which accelerator participation is only one (Hathaway 2016b; Van Weele 2016; Hallen et al. 2014). It is extremely difficult to disentangle success factors (CBIA 2016). As Sean Randolph, senior director of the Bay Area Council Economic Institute, states: "It is not necessarily the case that if a startup company gets venture investment, this is because they were in an accelerator. There may be a connection, but it shouldn't be assumed." Silicon Valley accelerator expert Susan Lucas-Conwell emphasizes that received funding is a meager indicator of startup performance success: "Raising money doesn't mean you are a successful business, it just means you have a longer runway."

Accelerators are embedded in the Silicon Valley network of support agencies, though the degree of cooperation varies. Some networks are institutionalized, while others are more loosely organized. Linking the outside world of investors, corporates, and technology stakeholders to the inside world of highly talented startups is a quality that all accelerators share, independent of their domain area, technology focus, or business model. It takes two to dance the Silicon Valley startup tango: investors looking for talent and talent looking for investors.

4 Strong Teams Will Win

How Accelerators Select and Coach Startup Teams

In this chapter, I examine how Silicon Valley accelerators recruit startup teams and the criteria they use to select new ventures. Is there consensus about the latent and manifest qualities that startup founders need to have to market their business idea and develop their company? Do accelerator executives favor founder teams over solo entrepreneurs? Furthermore, I present my main findings regarding the way accelerators make use of external mentors in coaching startups that participate in their programs. As will be shown, mentorship is a core characteristic of Silicon Valley's ecosystem.

Selection procedures

The way Silicon Valley accelerators recruit startups to participate in their growth programs varies but is generally highly selective. This is true for both general accelerators (high-volume/low-touch) and specialized/niche accelerators (low-volume/high-touch). And even most office-space-based accelerators apply rather strict admissions procedures. In this section, I outline the various admissions methods that accelerators use in taking on the most talented and promising startup entrepreneurs. An overwhelming majority of accelerators prefer startup teams over single startup entrepreneurs, as we shall see.

The larger, general/low-touch accelerators apply highly structured and routinized intake and selection methods that are online-based. 500 Startups accepts four batches per year (two in San Francisco and two in Mountain View) and receives 2,500+ startup applications per batch. "We do interviews with about 400 applicants, of which we accept about 40. So our acceptance rate is around two percent." (Elizabeth Yin). As the accelerator's website concludes: "It's tougher to get into 500 Startups than Harvard, MIT or Stanford." In terms of how startups are selected, Elizabeth explains: "We're looking for a complete team. A team that consists of what I call a 'hacker' and a 'hustler'. One is good in product development and one in customer acquisition. Secondly, the product is usually complete and there must be some traction. A typical startup that gets invited to interview is doing around $10K per month in revenue, recurring revenue." Roughly 30 percent of the selected startup teams are international.

Plug and Play, another large accelerator, reviews over 2,000 startup applications each year per accelerator program and invests in over 100. Saeed Amidi has a particular interest in first-time entrepreneurs "straight out of college". Why? "Because of a couple of reasons. One is they don't have much baggage, they don't have a house payment, they don't have kids to put through college. So they can work 70, 80 hours a week. Generally, they are more passionate, smarter I would say. And the third thing is: if you are younger, you can deliver it better. They don't think about failure as much. Failure is no option. Which is not to say that they don't fail but they are so optimistic and proactive, and that's what I enjoy the most."

About 400 startups are housed in the Plug and Play building in Sunnyvale, of which a substantial number are international teams. Saeed also prefers teams over solo founders: "The first two, three, four years are hard, very hard for a startup. I think you need the team spirit and give-and-take to go through this roller coaster phase." The strength of the team is Plug and Play's main selection criterion: "The team, the passion, the capability of building what they want to build, and the talent to pivot, to change as they go on."

The Alchemist Accelerator takes three batches of startups per year, receives about 300 applications per cohort, and accepts approximately 17 startups per batch, so their acceptance rate is about five to six percent. They make use of a panel of judges (composed of alumni, mentors, and CEOs) to validate the startups' business proposals. The selection criteria it uses, according to Danielle D'Agostaro, is "primarily team, technology and market opportunity, and whether a VC would back them or not. It's very rare that we take solo entrepreneurs. Startup life is very hard and it is extremely difficult for one person to take on all the roles that are associated with it. The team needs to be technically strong and business savvy." The age of team members varies but on average is late twenties and early thirties. "They tend to be in that early range where they are old enough to be wise and young enough to be dangerous. They are at that point in their lives where they think: 'if I'm going to do something I need to do it now' and that fire, that drives them." The Alchemist Accelerator also has a strong international outreach, with 40 percent of its startup classes coming from outside the U.S.

Founders Space in San Francisco admits startups on a rolling basis and gets over 1,000 applications a year. Co-founder Naomi Kokubo recounts: "We usually accept somewhere between 10 and 20 startups in our program here in Silicon Valley, two to four times a year. But we also bring our program over to various countries such as Taiwan, Korea, China and other countries. We also have our co-branded space in Shanghai. In those countries our partners will do most of the selection." Regarding the qualities that Founders Space is after: "Team is important, and we definitely want to have some technology element. The business has to be scalable, the market has to be big, and ideally there is already some traction." Naomi emphasizes the importance of team composition. "In the team we want someone who understands the business inside out, who knows their market, their customers, and is able to carry the company through. That's usually the CEO. We also want a technologist in the team, who understands the current technology and can actually build the product; and we want a design expert in the team who can make their product shine with greater user experience. And finally, it would be good to have someone who knows how to take their product to the market. It doesn't necessarily have to be four different people; the CEO could take on more than one role."

HAX aims to grow hardware companies and receives over 2,000 applications a year from which it selects 30 startups (spread over two batches). Selecting the best startup candidates is complicated according to Cyril Ebersweiler: "Because the hardware venture requires a very different scale and requires strong technical skills. But these skills are not what is going to make the venture successful. Our startup engineers will have to deal with suppliers, with manufacturers, with distributors. The communications aspect of the business is very important." The recruitment procedure is further complicated by the fact that participants spend almost six months in HAX's accelerator lab space in Shenzhen, China, to finalize their proto- type and grow the business. Cyril notes that HAX seldom accepts solo entrepreneurs: "It is very rare; especially in the hardware industry you need teams. You have to deal with design, mechanical engineering, marketing, sales, communications, etc."

TiE LaunchPad receives over 200 applications per batch for four to six slots. "We probably end up meeting with roughly 20 of those," according to Prashant Shah. In describing TiE's selection criteria, he says: "We are looking for the right idea, with the right market, and with the right team. We are investing money so we are looking for people who are dedicated to making the startup a success. We are doing enterprise, this generally requires some experience in industry. Most of the founders we talk to are first-time founders who left their jobs and somehow developed a great idea that might be an extension of what their company was doing or even something completely different." Prashant also prefers teams over solo entrepreneurs. "And they know that they need help in all aspects of company building, everything from just the basics to how to run a board meeting all the way to how they find customers, how they find investors and crossing that."

BootUP prides itself in creating a micro-ecosystem that combines all the good ingredients from the larger Silicon Valley ecosystem – "kind of the Amazon.com for startups" according to Marco ten Vaanholt. Finding startups that best fit the BootUP system is a major challenge. "So, we make time for everybody because that one ten-minute session could change their lives forever." Marco aims for a smart ratio of 70 percent serial entrepreneurs and 30 percent first-time entrepreneurs, the underlying idea being that the first group can transfer knowledge to the second group. BootUP also invests in post-seed startups "based on the core philosophy of does the project enhance life, would you use it in your home, and does it change the way you and I live?" Marco also favors teams. "Teams are very important in the startup world. The earlier the startup, the more important team is. What we are investing in is basically team and idea. And the main question is: is the team going to execute the idea or not?"

Accelerator expert Lucas-Conwell points at the role of team composition: "I think the most successful startup teams are balanced in terms of experience and profiles, knowledge of the industry they are in, and deep understanding of what the problem is that they are solving. (...) I think that just guys isn't healthy, just engineers isn't healthy, and just twenty-year olds isn't healthy either." Susan is a mentor to company teams that participate in StartX, the Stanford-affiliated accelerator. Executive team member Brian Hoffman tells me that StartX gets about 1,000 to 1,200 applications a year and its acceptance rate is between eight and twelve percent. The rate of what Brian calls "intentional sourcing" of later-stage Stanford startups is higher and close to 50 percent. The regular admissions procedure is a lengthy online application involving many questions about the founders, their background, funding raised, accomplishments, etc. Applications are screened by a panel of judges from the StartX mentor and alumni community and corporate partners. About half of the applicants survive the first round and are interviewed in eight-minute sessions, where the focus is on the founders' profile: "Are they passionate, are they committed, are they real entrepreneurs, will they walk through a wall, how does the founding team solve problems, what about team dynamics?" Half of them will come down again. The second round of interviews concentrates on the fit between the startup founders and the StartX community and culture, as well as the technical skill set. Like the other accelerators, StartX has a preference for founder teams. "We do take solo founders but anyone that applies as a solo founder there would at least be a flag raised and we will dig into the founder's track record as an entrepreneur."

The Babson College Summer Venture Program is very selective too, and accepts a maximum of fifteen teams. Applications are open to undergraduate and graduate students as well as to Babson college alumni. Recently, the program was expanded to Babson's branch in San Francisco. The acceptance rate is lower than 25 percent. Cindy Klein-Marmer adds: "We actually have created side programs to help support those entrepreneurs that did not get into our summer venture program because it is so selective." In evaluating applications, Cindy says: "We look at overall viability of the business idea, we look at traction, but at the core we look at team. We do accept solo entrepreneurs, which is unique compared to a venture-backed accelerator. In a way, our program is a precursor to such accelerators. We often will find folks building up their team while in our program, so having that ability for them to move with us and to understand who are the right team members and not just because they are classmates. So finding those folks who complement them, who feel their weaknesses." Among the teams is a considerable number of female-led startups.

Samsung NEXT's selection procedure directly flows from its growth philosophy "to find world-class entrepreneurs and help them grow their business from idea to product to scale", according to Gary Coover. Their recruitment focus is on experienced entrepreneurs "who have gone through startups before and have hit familiar barriers that they either weren't able to overcome or that they found to be incredibly difficult to overcome, and we can help them with that. Distribution is probable the best example. Samsung can really help here, as it provides access to the largest distribution platform in the world." Samsung NEXT does not do cohorts or running a formal curriculum. Samsung NEXT's chief selection criteria are: "Founding team, focus area, and market opportunity. Team: we want them to have experience together and success having built products before. Focus area: you can roughly call it frontier tech, e.g. AR, VR, machine learning, AI, data and analytics, autonomous vehicles and drones, IoT, that is probably a good start. And it is all software-focused. Finally, market opportunity: there must be a scalable market." There is no standardized application process, but the process itself is akin to the seed funding model of any other Silicon Valley investor.

Some of the smaller high-touch, domain-specific, and niche accelerators are even more restrictive than their larger counterparts. The Fabric is a good example: "We are selective, very selective. We often deal with founders that we already know, who maybe work for large companies. They might be in their early forties, have gone from engineer to a director, and suddenly have this urge and say: 'I have seen this done and my founders previously made money, I am doing very well, I've reached this stage and my kids are in college and my bills are paid, I would love to do something on my own.'"(Prem Talreja). For The Fabric, a good team and team culture are key too. "I'll tell them: you will spend more time together than you will with your spouses. You better demonstrate that you like each other, you better demonstrate you are complementing. You better sign up to this that divorce is not an option."

The Hive operates in a specific market with a strong focus on data-driven technologies. As a co-creation growth studio, it is not interested in massive numbers of applicants. Co-founder T.M. Ravi elucidates: "We are theme- and content-oriented. The main question is: what is the concept and is this a breakthrough concept? Does it lead to a large market? In The Hive, we build companies. We have the ability and resources to go out and find the best people in a particular domain and ask them to become a founder. Ultimately, we look for a unique concept targeting a large market and supported with a strong team with the ability to execute the concept." In terms of the qualities The Hive looks for in team members: "Our entrepreneurs need to have that scrappiness, that passion and zeal to succeed, it is part of their psyche."

Imagine H_2O, a non-profit niche accelerator, deliberately chooses to focus on a limited number of startups per year – ten to twelve – out of some 90-100 applications. Besides written material, applicants also submit a three-minute video in which they pitch their idea, team, and market strategy. Water experts are brought in to act as judges to look for evidence of market share, market segmentation, the pain point the team wants to solve, product-market fit, and the startup's go-to-market policy. Tom Ferguson expounds: "One of the big things in water entrepreneurship is that there are lots of engineers who are fantastic at engineering but aren't brilliant in the nuts-and-bolts kind of building and selling a business." And it is precisely the ability to communicate that is extremely important. To which Tom's colleague Nimesh Modak adds: "Because if you can't sell your idea, no one is going to do that for you. Founder sales are incredibly important, especially in this business." Imagine H_2O takes solo entrepreneurs but, as Tom emphasizes: "Solo is tough and should be tough. It sure is tough to sell to investors if you are a solo entrepreneur. Team is critical."

Powerhouse is another high-touch, niche accelerator, one that is focused on accelerating solar startups. It takes four companies per cohort, and two cohorts per year. The selection procedure is invite-only. Emily Kirsch: "We invite about a dozen startups out of about 40-50 that are on our radar and have expressed interest, and we bring that down to four companies that will do the program." Powerhouse's selection criteria are based on the 'three T' model: total addressable market, team, and technology. The order is vital according to Emily: "Because you can have the best team and the best technology in the world, but if nobody is going to buy your product, if there is no market opportunity for it, then it doesn't matter." Innovativeness is what Powerhouse is looking for, or what Emily calls "startups that are ahead of their time." The ideal setup, according to her, is a CEO and a CTO, "and then, as they are with us, they can grow further teams from there."

Cleantech Open receives between 200 and 250 applications a year and uses similar selection criteria. Ian Foraker notes that: "We look at team, technology, and market, and we have panels of volunteer judges who evaluate the applicants." He estimates Cleantech Open's rejection rate to be about 50 percent. And experience has taught the accelerator not to accept solo founders: "We have a rule that individuals are not allowed in our program. We found that among individual entrepreneurs, the chance they drop out or fail is much higher."

At Women's Startup Lab, a good example of a niche accelerator, the mission is to grow female entrepreneurs and help them build their business. It accepts nine women per cohort and runs three to four batches a year. Total applications are between 170 to 200 a year, although at the moment I interviewed CEO Ari Horie the accelerator was in the midst of a rebranding process and those numbers had fallen to around 80. Ari clarifies the target group of her lab: "As we are founder-centric, it is important that female entrepreneurs who want to participate in our program are open, coachable, super-talented, stand the power of our *hito* philosophy, want to be part of our collaborative, believe in giving back to the community, and see themselves as role models for the next generation." Ari underlines the importance of founder qualities such as tenacity, coachability, and authenticity to drive ideas, performance, and success. "We don't believe in just money." With regard to teams versus solo founders, Ari has an interesting perspective. "We at Women's Startup Lab want to be the founders' champion; we want to be the village to support female entrepreneurs. There are unique invisible challenges that women founders face, and we relentlessly try to find solutions. We train our founders to overcome these challenges so that they can focus on building their startups rather than dealing with societal and cultural issues that hold back women leaders to succeed. The whole point is creating the formula that works for women." The Startup Lab focuses on empowering individual female entrepreneurs rather than on teams.

In my interviews, I also asked accelerating platforms how they select their tenants. GSVlabs' startup selection process is network-based. Marlon

Evans: "We do no outbound marketing. All of our startups come to us from referrals through our mentor network and our investor network. We are a little bit later stage and look for companies that have some seed funding, some traction in the market, which gives us external validation of their product. We look at the people, the product, the potential, the opportunity, and the predictability of the revenue." Mindset is critical, too. "We are only as strong as our community. If you don't have that kind of open willingness to share with others, then likely you are not going to be successful here." GSVlabs' entry policy is a rolling admissions and selection process that boils down, according to Marlon, to two questions: "Do we think the startup is a good fit and do we have space?" It recruits internationally, with over 20 countries represented.

Runway, the San-Francisco-based incubator and co-working space, looks at fit and entrepreneurial qualities. Matt Walters notes, "We have to be very successful about who we bring in here because they are affecting everyone else. People with a good attitude because we are all working at open spaces. We look for entrepreneurs we think are going to be successful. Team, attitude, background, product, traction, investors, are all important criteria." Regarding teams versus solo entrepreneurs, Runway is very explicit: "Usually it is individuals who have ideas but teams who have businesses." Runway gets about five to ten applications a week and admits around ten percent of its applicants.

Prospect Silicon Valley is a technology demonstration center that receives about 75 applications a year; the rejection rate is around 60-75%. Founder Doug Davenport points out that his clients "need to have credible technology, financial stability, leadership skills. (...) We're not evaluating them as potential investment but on how compelling their solution is, how this is going to be perceived by stakeholders, by venture investors, and by the public. Is it a company we can work with? Can we help them? We don't do batches or program cohorts. Each of our companies is unique." Prospect's admittance policy applies three selection criteria: applications must fit their area of focus and have a prototype ready for customer demonstration, and the technology must be focused on B2B or business-to-government markets.

Hacker Dojo's model is based on co-working space and low-cost membership. True to its image and cultural background, it has an open non-restrictive admission policy, as Jun Wong emphasizes: "There is no selection process or judgment. You just sign up online. It's a self-service system. It's an open source, it's a shared space. We don't even have fixed desks."

At RocketSpace, founder and CEO Duncan Logan was forced to pivot the admissions policy in order to cope with the abundance of startups approaching the accelerator. "We get over 35 applications a week, so we needed to make the selection process a lot easier. The rule is: 'if you haven't raised funding, then you're too early'. So if you are invested in by Andreessen or Sequoia or Greylock, great VCs or great angels, then we're like: 'well, that's easy, you're straight in.'" RocketSpace clearly leans towards selecting startup teams over solo founders: "It's all teams. (...) You need an impressive, exceptional CEO. You need an impressive leader. You need an exceptional team, a very motivated team." Or, as written on RocketSpace's website: "Isolation is not an option."

To conclude, Silicon Valley accelerators are very selective in their admissions policies. This holds true for for-profit as well as non-profit accelerators, for general as well as domain-specific and niche accelerators, and for low-touch as well as high-touch accelerators. In most cases, the recruitment criteria are clear: strong team, strong technology, ample market opportunity. Having traction also helps. There appears to be a general consensus about the importance of teams in startups ventures. Startups that lack a strong team will simply not survive, even with great technology, even with great market prospects. As Reid Hoffman, co-founder and former chairman of LinkedIn, summarizes: "Everyone in the entrepreneurial community agrees that assembling a talented team is as important as it gets." (Hoffman & Casnocha 2012: 83)

Mentoring

The coaching offered by Silicon Valley accelerators is one of their most salient and most consistent features. Mentors are typically serial entrepreneurs – often former startup founders – who have the right experience, competences, and networks to coach startup teams in the early and very challenging phase of their new venture. They know the pitfalls and frustrations of founding a startup and its numerous trials. Effective mentors speak the startup's business language and are able to identify with the founders' way of thinking. They have "been there, done that". They know the hard times.

Nearly all of my interviewees are startup mentors in their accelerators, either as executives of their mentoring programs or as one-to-one mentors to the startups participating in their accelerator. This last role is particularly prevalent among the smaller accelerators. A good example is Tandem, the hardware and software accelerator focused on mobile. Sunil Bhargava describes it thus: "You can think of us as extending your team; we'll be part of your team. It's not only about advice, it's about execution; we get our hands dirty."

The same is true for The Hive, where T.M. Ravi explains: "We collaborate with our entrepreneurs to really add management and entrepreneurial bandwidth to the startup team. It is important that the startup founders become the soul of the company. They are the ones that have to run the company 24/7 for the next many years, and we can only advise, mentor, and guide them. That's our role." Prem Talreja at The Fabric, compares startup team mentoring to the parent-children relationship: "It's like children, right? Initially they are dependent on you for everything, and then they get to the age that they want to be on their own and leave home."

Experienced startup mentors are the pillars of an accelerator's micro-ecosystem, and there appears to be no shortage of them. The Silicon Valley mentor pool is impressive. Co-founder and managing partner Marco ten Vaanholt of BootUP reveals: "We have access to over 800 serial entrepreneurs. They are always on the lookout for their next grade and get to work with the startup for about six months. They might complement the team if they feel there is a good match and that they can help scale up the company. We also look at how we can complement the startup with additional executive talent. To beef up the executive team is good for two reasons. One is the experience and knowledge factor; the second is on becoming more investable. It's all about 'de-risking' the investment at all times."

TiE LaunchPad also makes use of a large supply of mentors: "We have roughly 350 mentors in our organization. Part of our six-month curriculum is that we allow our startups to pick their mentor. During the time they are in the program they have a dedicated one-to-one mentor they can rely on. Between the mentor and myself we figure out what the resources are to draw through the TiE network." (Prashant Shah). Mentors may be former entrepreneurs but also former investors. Says Prashant: "A lot of our mentors were actually investors themselves, either as angels or as VCs. TiE has been doing mentorship for 20+ years."

The Alchemist Accelerator also draws from a substantial mentor pool. Danielle D'Agostaro: "We have over four, five hundred mentors in our network. Most of them are all doing it pro bono; they are doing it because they want to give back, work with the startups, get their name out there as a tough expert to the startup community, and so they use the Alchemist as that channel."

StartX recruits its volunteer mentors from Stanford faculty and alumni: "Our optional mentoring programs take at a high level with different forms. One is that we called our lead mentors. Those are serial entrepreneurs that have seen the arc of at least two companies as a founding member. They are startup team coaches that are there to help with co-founder issues, the loneliness of starting a new company, and with coping with day-today business pressure. It's the closest type of mentoring. The second type of mentoring we do is company mentoring. Startups get a mark board of advisors during the 10-week program period and they meet with them in board style. Members are called advisors. So, mentors are here to help you as a person, advisors are here to help you as a company. And the final type of mentoring is experts: people in our Stanford network that are domain specialists."(Brian Hoffman).

The Babson College accelerator is embedded in a firm coaching environment. Says Cindy Klein-Marmer: "We have dedicated mentors and dedicated advisors at each stage in our accelerator and those are traditionally adjunct faculty or full-time faculty here at Babson, very much on a part-time basis but it's an active role that they are playing." Internal Babson advisors are financially compensated; mentors are not. External mentors play a significant role in the Babson accelerator. As Cindy clarifies: "Mentors are not paid and so we end up getting a lot of external mentors who are volunteering both because of their own interest, intrinsic value and reward that they are getting out of it but also because of a desire to get more engaged with Babson."

Startup 500 has an interesting internal coaching scheme. Its program is on accelerating development and growth, and it creates an in-house 'distribution team' consisting of previous marketers and sales people. Elizabeth Yin explains: "We pair every company with someone from this distribution team for setting up, for instance, an outbound sales process, or we pair them with an online marketing expert. We give every startup two coaches: one on customer acquisition and one on fundraising. These coaches are paid for, they are on our payroll, but they can be fired at any time. The idea is that these coaches help our companies to grow during the four-month program. Ideally, a company comes in here and they can double or triple their revenue in this period. That's a great story for fundraising, of course." Careful pairing, according to Elizabeth, is essential. "Not every coach is going to be a good fit for every company." A good accelerator reputation also helps, of course, to attract mentors. Naomi Kokubo of Founders Space admits that "it is very fortunate that Founders Space is well known. We get a lot of people asking to be a mentor."

Finding the right match between mentor and founder teams is crucial. As accomplished startup mentor and Silicon Valley expert Susan Lucas-Conwell asserts: "There needs to be a match in personality. There needs to be an openness on the part of the startup team to be really interested in mentorship, otherwise it is a waste of time. There needs to be mutually agreed-upon added value. Where I can generally provide value is around business strategy, strategic partnerships, and working place culture. I have mentored consumer goods companies, digital health companies, not-for-profits. And I have a long history of mentoring women's startups." Why is mentoring important to Susan? "I am interested in new developments. Keeps you sharp. Interesting startups that maybe one day will grow. (...) It is not necessarily about raising money, it is about 'wow, they've got their act together'. They have actually moved forward, they have progressed. So, from whenever I started and wherever I ended, they've actually moved forward." Seeing startups grow is clearly a gratifying experience.

Ari Horie of Women's Startup Lab emphasizes the need for the right match between her mentors and the mission of her accelerator. She focuses on building a team of advisors and mentors with real-world entrepreneurial experience. "Some consultants only have a theoretical understanding by being around startups but they have never been an entrepreneur. Nine out of ten of our mentors and advisors are serial entrepreneurs or investors themselves. They understand how hard it is to start and run a business and the challenges that founders face. They also have an amazing network and they mentor female founders because they want to make a difference. They want women to be successful. They believe in you." Women's Startup Lab has both female and male mentors. Ari shares an intriguing observation in this respect: "I noticed that 95% of our male mentors have a daughter."

The mission-driven Cleantech Open accelerator works with assigned mentors from a pool of about 250 volunteers. Ian Foraker, executive director, states that "we have a great mentorship culture in the Bay Area. The value of the mentorship is proportional to the richness of the ecosystem. It's really robust. So it's easier to get volunteer mentors here. They are contributing, giving back, helping an important cause." Much of Cleantech Open's mentoring is by mentor calls coupled with one-to-one business clinics, bootcamps, and webinars. "Mentors may be nearly retired, subject-matter experts; they may be in current transition; they may be consultants. They are asked to sign up between two to four hours a week over the course of the summer to meet with their startups teams."

For Imagine H_2O, mentoring is a crucial part of their accelerator program; "coachability is key" according to Nimesh Modak. "We have a core group of mentors that have been doing it year after year. They have very specific skill sets that match up to our mission. They dedicate probably ten to twelve hours a year. It all comes back to our mission. They look at what we are doing and say: you know what, you are right. Water is crazy, difficult, but terribly important. We get constantly requests from people to join our judging panel." Colleague Tom Ferguson explains what it is that mentors offer: "They take the process of starting a company very seriously. And that's everything from improving your pitch act, to how you are feeling as head of a new company, and let's talk through some of the human stuff that's going on, the pressure, cash flow issues, the need to deal with investors, making difficult hiring decisions, firing people. All the stuff that keeps startup founders up at night."

Powerhouse, another niche accelerator, has a mentorship model based on facilitating linkages through network events. Emily Kirsch: "By organizing workshops, signature events, guest speaker presentations, we give our startups every opportunity to meet a potential mentor, and we let the mentor decide who they want to work with. There is a lot to be said for people self-selecting who they want to engage with on an ongoing basis. Everyone is adult, everyone is really ambitious, and that's why they are here in the first place."

Accelerators that are primarily focused on creating an inspiring environment for startups and some basic facilities – e.g. based on an office-renting model – have a looser, more informal mentor approach. Hacker Dojo is a good example. Jun Wong notes that "the process is quite organic, similar to how Sand Hill Road or downtown Mountain View came about. We try to make this an open space where people can come in. Mentors will naturally be around. We are very early stage. When teams are ready for the next stage, they'll use other services in the Valley. There is a lot of mentorship in this area."

Marlon Evans of GSVlabs calls volunteering mentorship "the secret sauce of Silicon Valley". He goes on to explain: "We have 130 mentors that have all signed up to volunteer. They are not being compensated for their time, they just want to pay it forward because somebody helped them along their career too and they want to help others. We ask for two or three hours per month." It is not all altruism, of course. "Some of them have gone to spend a lot more time, become advisors, get equity in the company. But that's all up to them." Mentor recruiting is not a real challenge for GSVlabs: "We have no issue in finding mentors. For some niche areas, we may need to do some scouting. In fact, companies come to us and say, hey, we are an IT company, and we have employees that would love to be helpful to your community."

Runway has similar experiences. Matt Walters relates that "I find it is relatively easy to get someone to be a mentor. A lot of it comes down to commitment level. Some mentors have a dedicated station here in Runway and they are helping teams organically. Some come in once a month, stay with us for some time and have office hours. We post it on to everybody, and startup teams sign up for meeting with the mentor and work with them. I think it works well. We are not over-burning the mentors. It's all on a voluntary basis." Matt is a mentor himself, for example as a coach for startups teams that are fundraising. "We will sit down, go through their pitch deck, slide by slide. (...) VCs see so many deals that are constantly pitched that you really need to get to the point of your value proposition immediately. In the first 30 seconds you earn the next five minutes of their attention."

Pitching is important in the early stage, while sales determine a startup's survival chance. Effective accelerator mentorship centers around customer response and take-up. Sunil Bhargava of Tandem is clear about what he thinks is the most important factor: "In one sentence: it's all about getting traction. The first thing is to sit down and really define some clear metrics that are going to be measured, to try some experiments that will lead to proof or disproof of the thesis whether to go to market. We first try to estab-lish demand. Often what we find is that the cost of acquiring customers is too high or the experiments aren't quite right. Then we have to go back to the drawing board and say okay it is a small change or it is really short and does not work." Sunil's mentoring method very much resembles the lean startup model developed by Eric Ries described in chapter 2.

Silicon Valley accelerators, in short, are all about mentoring. This conclu-sion is aptly put by Duncan Logan of RocketSpace: "The Valley ecosystem, you know, is such that here everyone, everyone is a sort of mentor."

Conclusion

Taking a helicopter view, it becomes clear from my findings that stringent selection and close mentoring are key ingredients of the success formula of Silicon Valley startup accelerators. The admission bar is set high, and founder coaching is pivotal. Selectivity and mentor involvement are funda-mental accelerator characteristics. The smaller, for-profit accelerators are most selective in their admissions policy, and they excel in hands-on startup coaching. Getting into a highly selective and reputed accelerator is a great launch pad and increases a startup's chances for next-stage funding. How do accelerators select? The short answer is: team, technology, and market. Most accelerator executives look for strong teams with complementary founder skill sets as well as passion, drive, energy, and perseverance. Accelerators favor founder teams over solo entrepreneurs, as they believe that growing a startup is a team effort. A good fit between technology and market is absolutely imperative. The better the scaling opportunities, the higher the startup's chances of being admitted to the accelerator program.

The smoothly operating mentor system at Silicon Valley accelerators amazes many European visitors. Giving back to the community, in this case to the startup community, is part of the Valley's DNA. All my interviewees state that finding mentors is not a problem. Most of them are experienced entrepreneurs, many of whom have founded several startups. The large pool of mentors and coaches is remarkable, and in the early startup phase they offer their services for free. It would be naive, however, to conclude that the mentor system is purely altruistic. Mentors have an incentive to be linked to promising startups with scaling potential. Still, the entrepreneurial force of the prevailing Silicon Valley culture of voluntary mentoring is extraordinary.

5   Working on a Dream

Accelerator Startup Programs

In this chapter, I describe and analyze the main features of the Silicon Valley accelerator programs, particularly with respect to their nature, content, and structure. I take a closer look at the frequency, intensity, and duration of the different accelerator programs and the way they are organized. The descriptions and analysis provide a broad insight into the operational fundamentals of a wide variety of accelerator approaches and programs. As in the previous chapters, I first look at general/low-touch accelerators before moving on to the more domain-specific and niche/high-touch accelerators, and finally accelerating platforms.

In spite of obvious differences in approach, focus, and strategy, all Silicon Valley accelerators underline the importance of selective admissions, strong founder teams, passion, the ability to think big, scalability, and growth.

General accelerators

500 Startups is one of the most renowned high-volume, cohort-based general accelerators in Silicon Valley. It offers a four-month program to admitted startup teams. Classes work with designated mentors on business strategy, product development, business growth, investor pitches, and customer acquisition. 500 Startups runs four classes a year, with 40-50 teams per cohort, and is now into batch 20 (as of spring 2017). It offers programs and in-house working space in Mountain View, San Francisco, and Mexico City. Startup teams come from over 20 countries, and more than 500 companies have graduated since 2010. Elizabeth Yin sums up the program's essence as: "Traction and scalability. Our programs focus on optimizing prospective customer interaction and how to scale up the existing process. Successful growth is really about managing the details of these approaches." These details are highly operational and functional. "Do teams write the right emails to customers? Do they send 'cold' emails? Do they make enough phone calls to potential customers? Do they try different interactions?" These are important practical questions that are systematically raised by founder team coaches, according to Elizabeth. So is sharing and feedback. "We ask our founder teams in our weekly batch meetings to share their problems, their fears – issues that keep them awake. Being a founder is very

lonely. The teams in their batch are the best people for them to rely on, as they are going through the same challenges."

Plug and Play also organizes cohort-based programs for startup teams but over a 12-week period. Cohort size differs somewhat, depending on the technology vertical. In 2016, it accelerated over 300 startups. This high-volume accelerator houses over 400 teams, many of which rent longer-term office space. Programs focus on business development, on fine-tuning business models and marketing challenges, and on connecting startup teams to entrepreneurial experts and VCs. Plug and Play provides admitted startups access to its infrastructure and on-site data center, logistical support, networking events, mentorship, corporate introductions, startup-corporate engagement sessions, executives-in-residence, and introductions to investors. Achieving a good team-product-customer-investor fit is an essential part of Plug and Play's accelerator programs. Saeed Amidi, Plug and Play's founder and CEO, explains: "After we choose the best team, the best ideas, the best startups, we will introduce them to the corporate partners and venture capitalists in our network." Plug and Play puts a lot of effort into creating a dynamic entrepreneurial vibe in its Sunnyvale accelerator offices. Visitors from all over the world come and go. After my interview with Saeed, the CEO of a large Japanese electronics company and his entourage came in to say hello and shake hands.

The Alchemist Accelerator offers six-month programs, three times a year (overlapping classes), to a maximum of 17 teams. As of early 2017, it had organized a total of 14 batches. The Alchemist's primary focus is on seed-stage enterprise startups, and its accelerator program centers on business model innovation, leadership, customer development, direct and online marketing and sales, market validation, and fundraising. There are weekly gatherings, lectures, workshops, roundtables, networking events, and brokered customer meetings. Program events are optional (except Demo Day). The gatherings organized are based on input from the Alchemist's advisor faculty, guest lectures, VCs, and customer networks. Teaching skills and mentoring startup teams are standard elements of the program. Partner and COO Danielle D'Agostaro: "We do put [startups] in front of VCs, we do put them in front of customers, teach them how to pitch to both." The Alchemist's unique system of overlapping classes has advantages, as Danielle clarifies: "Learning during overlapping classes changes. In the beginning, teams are learning about sales, and at the end, teams are learning about fundraising. While they are learning about fundraising, a new class is starting to learn about sales. We are constantly going through these stages back and forth. The teams coming in can see what the future looks like, and the ones going out can coach the incoming teams. So there is a bit of internal mentoring. Big brother, big sister kind of thing." Demo Day is the apotheosis of many accelerator programs. In the case of the Alchemist, it includes startup team pitches of a maximum of four minutes and a one-minute introduction by a lead customer, given to a large audience of investors.

Founders Space has a different philosophy and offers a combined incubator and accelerator program. The program is an intensive two-week program filled with classes, workshops, and lectures every day, culminating in investor Pitch Day. Its online incubator program provides three months of remote access to hundreds of startup video lessons and business materials. The accelerator program includes mentoring and training that zero in on participating startups' business model, product-market fit, launch and marketing plan, traction, scalability, and pitch presentations. When asked if two weeks might not be a little short, Naomi Kokubo responds: "We have done a four-week program many times but we found that a two-week program works well, especially for our overseas teams. It is a very demanding, dynamic, and interactive program, with lots of one-on-one feedback moments." The program ends with Pitch Day, where startup teams pitch to an audience of investors that includes angels, VCs, and corporate investors. Founders Space works with batches of about 10-20 startup teams.

Samsung NEXT has coaching activities similar to a corporate startup accelerator. Their approach is to grow early-stage software startups into scalable businesses that impact the Samsung ecosystem and can ultimately help Samsung foster an energetic corporate startup culture. The broader Samsung NEXT organization has a single focus: to build, grow, and scale software startups. It has a strong preference for experienced founders, which Gary Coover, head of global operations, justifies by explaining: "Part of that is we are not rigidly programmatic. When startups come in here, it is not like we are running a curriculum with classes all the time. We have a series of resources and a pool of deep domain experts that they can leverage. But the resources are there for each startup to leverage as they see fit. We offer services that are customized to fit the startup, not a rigid program. We are flexible and focus on the individual teams." As mentioned in chapter 3, Samsung NEXT Start offers a seed funding model and an in-residence model. Collectively, the models aim to boost innovation for Samsung. "Our mandate", says Gary, "is to invest in areas that might be a couple of years ahead of where Samsung currently is, to stay in tune with groundbreaking new technologies and partner with tech innovators."

TiE LaunchPad is a smaller general accelerator for enterprise startups. Mentors are charter members of TiE Silicon Valley. It accepts four to eight B2B startups per batch for a five-month program. Mentors work on a weekly basis with founder teams during the program. The program consists of a curriculum of workshops, events, and speaker sessions covering sales, marketing, hiring, financials, and fundraising. There is a strong emphasis on pricing models and business strategy. Mentoring is a major program feature, as managing director Prashant Shah points out. "One of the unique things that we do is we allow startups to pick their mentor from the 350 mentors we have. We work with a dedicated mentor model." The program itself is very one-on-one – a workshop-oriented curriculum. "The basics, really. How to position your company, how to do presentations, how to get customers. And there is a lot of practice, a lot of interaction. We videotape founder presentations and pitches, and give them immediate feedback." TiE LaunchPad organizes a Demo Day at the end of the program, but this should not inhibit participating startups from raising funds earlier on in the program.

Hardware accelerator HAX admits a total of 30 startups per year in two batches. The accelerator's technology focus is on lifestyle and consumer electronics, robotics, health, infrastructure, and new materials. It offers a program where admitted teams relocate to HAX's office and lab space in Shenzhen, China to finalize their prototype and learn how to scale their business. Why the relocation? Founder and managing director Cyril Ebersweiler argues that there are a number of unique competitive advantages. In Shenzhen, startup teams are close to in-house prototype production, which is critical for hardware development. The metropolitan area (with a population of over 18 million) provides access to a massive pool of very cost-conscious and experienced engineers. China, furthermore, represents a huge B2B and B2C market, and HAX is located right in the heart of global electronics and manufacturing: Hua Qiang Bei. And going to Shenzhen, finally, is an exceptional cultural experience. Cyril, who lived in Asia for more than 15 years and speaks Chinese fluently, illustrates these advantages with a telling example: "Say you build a robot. Robots can have 10,000 pieces inside, it needs to be manufactured. If you manufacture a robot anywhere else in the world, it is going to cost you millions of dollars; in Shenzhen, we build robots with 1,000 bucks and we sell them for 2,000 bucks. What do we do? We create new markets because we managed to reduce the cost; but it is not costing alone, it is using the scale of existing elements, the supply chain of manufacturing." A different economy of scale is, in short, one of the main advantages of being relocated to China. "The other thing that happened was that because we're in Shenzhen, our alumni started to come back to do the manufacturing and then to do the second product. It became some kind of a base where people were gravitating around, and that was perfect. Our alumni became our mentors. And we grew. That is why we've moved our office actually every year." In just four years, HAX has expanded from a 100-square-meter office to 4,500 square meters.[68] HAX is all about solid mentoring. Founder teams meet weekly with their mentors to discuss strategy, prototype, supply chain management, distribution, etc. The final two weeks are spent in San Francisco on perfecting the investor pitch at HAX Demo Day Showcase.

BootUP offers three types of accelerator programs as part of its eco-system-based range of startup growth facilities and services: the general accelerator, the vertical accelerator, and the customized accelerator. The general accelerator is a three-month program aimed at launching and growing U.S. and international startups through educational sessions, tech talks, workshops, hands-on mentoring, site visits, and Demo Day pitches to VCs. The vertical accelerator links startups to specific corporate technology interests. Its program length varies but depends on the stage of proof-of-concept integration with sponsoring corporate partners. The customized accelerator, finally, is a two-year targeted growth program for selected startups and is a follow-up to the general and vertical accelerator. The program is high-touch, with five to ten mentors "bringing different expertise along a startup's growth journey," as the program description states. These targeted accelerator programs service a wide variety of startup and corporate needs. As Marco ten Vaanholt claims, "For each one of them we have different kind of avenues to educate them appropriately. (...) The teachings that we provide to help startups accelerate can simultaneously be taught to corporates, can be taught to the innovators, can even be taught to foreign trade delegations that visit Silicon Valley."

StartX and the Babson College Butler Venture Program are two, not-for-profit, general accelerators developed within universities. StartX offers a ten-week program three times a year to accepted founder teams from the Stanford University network. The program consists of four pillars: community, mentoring, education, and resources. The community pillar is based on building trusted professional relationships. Brian Hoffman, vice president of revenue, explains the vocabulary and approach: "Every other week we bring in our startups for two events. One is what we call our industry 'neighborhoods': we separate our startups by industry and stage. We surround them by their peers from that space (e.g., hardware, medical, enterprise). The space itself is run by Stanford alumni. The prime focus is on getting people together to work on shared problems. This flows right into the second 'neighborhood' which is topic-centered, e.g., marketing, sales, technical challenges." The idea behind the two neighborhoods is professional network building, problem sharing, and solution identification. It empowers starting entrepreneurs and enhances their social capital through access to the Stanford community. "To force people to come together is the only thing we force. To come together and share their struggling so that at the end of the program they are like, wow, I have all these Stanford people that I can call on, and they stay engaged with their community for the rest of their professional lives." StartX does not offer a structured or mandatory curriculum, but through its Stanford mentor system and embedded neighborhood models it provides a one-to-one approach as well as targeted workshops to meet specific founder needs.

The Babson College Butler Venture Accelerator Program helps Babson students and alumni to build, launch, and scale their new business. The program recently expanded to Babson's San Francisco campus. Fifteen teams are selected to enter the Summer Venture Program, a ten-week intensive experience to accelerate startup growth from ideation to launch, from minimum viable product (MVP) to scale. The program offers housing, workspace, meals, hands-on mentoring and advice, a speaker series, workshops, lunch and learn sessions, and other resources. "The ten weeks are incredibly intensive," according to Cindy Klein-Marmer, associate director of the accelerator program. "There is a constant focus on traction. The program is really about sales and marketing. The other pillar is a strong emphasis on community and accountability. We teach them how to lead and manage. We are training for real life." Students get regular feedback from angel investors during the program. "Students love that – a highly sought experience." The program culminates in the Summer Venture Showcase at which founder teams present their new business, their accomplishments, and their results to investors, industry innovators, and the Babson community.

Specialized accelerators

The domain-specific, smaller, for-profit accelerators provide intensive ('high-touch') launch and growth programs but not in the cohort-structured way that is typical of high-volume, low-touch accelerators. The Hive, the data-driven co-creation studio, is a good representative of such high-touch accelerators. As T.M Ravi explains: "The Hive is a venture studio that creates companies. There are three ways in which we do that and we call them co-creation models. In the first case, we come up with a concept or idea and we validate that concept. We decide to fund this concept and we recruit co-founders and the rest of the startup team. A second case is that we embrace an early-stage founding team, typically less than five people, and work with them to build their company. The third case is that we collaborate with a partner corporation (e.g., GE, Verizon, EMC) to develop companies from scratch." In each case, The Hive works very closely with founding teams in a hands-on operational way until the startup gets to the next round of funding (typically a series A round). "We lend our expertise, our experience, and our networks to drive momentum and value in these companies."

The Fabric has a comparable vision but a different technology focus: cloud-based networking technologies. Prem Talreja, vice president of marketing, underlines the active and one-on-one way in which The Fabric coaches admitted startups and entrepreneurs, which has two sides: "We may own a significant part of the companies we fund, but we are absolute equals. We will roll up our sleeves to reduce the risk of failure. We are mentor, coach, and partner. We want to make sure that founder teams make use of us. If not, we will step in. We owe that to our shareholders." The Fabric's hands-on approach is to accelerate the process from an initial concept to a company, helping the new company to polish its product, to validate it with prospective customers and partners, and to develop a viable business model. Through this collaboration model, it works towards bringing the company to the next funding stage.

Tandem is another smaller, high-touch accelerator targeting both hardware and software startups particularly in the field of mobile technology. Its accelerator studio and hardware prototyping lab is also based on the principle of active involvement to help startups grow. Tandem's founder and managing partner Sunil Bhargava summarizes the philosophy: "To take whatever business they have and refine it, take whatever product they have and refine it. To go from a plan for traction to actually demonstrated traction." In Sunil's long experience as an entrepreneur, mentor, and coach, accelerated early startup growth is all about product-market fit, fine-tuning, execution, traction, and team skills. And those keywords are the core of Tandem's accelerator activities. In Sunil's words: "The biggest thing is the importance of looking beyond your product. What is your business, what is the problem you are solving, who are your users, who are your customers, who is going to fund the product? It's not about taking risk, it's about understanding and removing risk."

I next move to the four smaller (non-profit and for-profit) niche accelerators that center on specific problem areas or target groups: Cleantech

Open, Imagine H_2O, Powerhouse, and Women's Startup Lab. Cleantech Open's mission is to launch and grow early-stage clean technology businesses by organizing a six-month training program (May to November) for accepted startup teams who spend about two to eight hours per week on program activities. The program is run by volunteer mentors, backed up by Cleantech Open's regional and national professionals, and involves business clinics, webinars, workshops, speaker sessions, investor meetings, startup-corporate matching, a three-day boot camp, and showcasing. Activities vary in focus, specificity, and fit. Ian Foraker: "The business clinics, for instance, are very one-on-one; they are about expanding your network, getting insight into particular startup issues. The workshops are more didactic, e.g. on marketing, customer profiling, funding." Some events are regional, others are national. Ian compares Cleantech Open's accelerator program to a multilayered cake consisting of different coatings. Data collection (customer discovery) is the foundation on which everything else is built. Structured dialogue (mentoring) is next and leverages the information collected through customer discovery. This is followed by clinics and networking events that offer additional perspectives and connections to a broad community. Webinars and workshops provide instruction in the key questions and issues that startups have. And the top layer is the showcasing – the expo, connections with investors (investor speed-dating), and the pitch competition. At several fixed moments in the program, startup teams will meet up. This allows them to become a group of peers – "a Cleantech community with a shared feeling that continues way after the program ends."

The core activity of Imagine H_2O, another non-profit, is to help its accepted startups bring to market their smart, data-driven solutions to short and long-term water issues. It offers a virtual, ten-month global program that provides water startup founder teams access to industrial, agricultural, and municipal customers, stakeholders, and investors in the water industry. Programs have topics that vary on a yearly basis such as water conservation, wastewater, food and agriculture, water efficiency, and water data. The focus is on building and scaling successful water startups. The program starts with a weeklong boot camp in San Francisco, and over the next months mentors help teams remotely with product refinement, marketing, funding, visibility, cash-flow management, organizational pressures, and team issues. Customer introductions are a salient part of the program, as Tom Ferguson notes: "We are very explicit about that. We offer our startup companies access to an expanding network of industry customers who agreed to have a look at our listed companies. If there is a fit, they will meet."

Later on in the program, similar introductions will be arranged with the investor community. When asked whether remote support isn't by definition limited, director Modak responds: "Not at all. You can have almost as much impact remotely as you can do in person. Besides, we see a company three times during the program. Sticking to ten to twelve startups a year, we are able to offer a personalized approach." There is no structured Demo Day, but showcasing occurs at the annual conferences of the American Water Works Association and the Water Environment Federation.

Powerhouse is a for-profit, high-touch, niche accelerator focused on launching and growing solar startups. What are the main ingredients of its six-month program? Emily Kirsch, co-founder and CEO, answers: "Promotion, technology, and money. Powerhouse is building a brand and reputation space, which opens doors for our startups. Solar is a very specific niche technology that will change the world. Funding is obviously essential; we offer our startups access to a variety of investors." Powerhouse organizes signature events, workshops, guest lectures, and investor speed-dating and brings in industry leaders, angel investors, VCs, and seasoned serial entrepreneurs. Startups work from Powerhouse's 24/7 co-working office space in downtown Oakland in the East Bay area. Mentors and experts provide feedback on the startups' progress and business strategy. Milestones and deliverables are standard program requirements. Emily: "I will meet with the startup teams every week to go over deliverables for that week to hold them accountable and provide some structure in running a company. Running a startup is a very amorphous endeavor." Powerhouse works hard on creating a dynamic accelerator culture, for example by hosting a weekly Open House event for founder teams. "We talk about what they are working on, anything they are struggling with that the group might be able to help with. It really builds camaraderie and willingness to collaborate."

The motto at Women's Startup Lab is: "Together we rewrite the code for female entrepreneurial success." This is quite a statement. Ari Horie, founder and CEO, argues that Silicon Valley traditionally is a very male-dominated culture, with subtle and not-so-subtle gender prejudices. She wants to address these preconceptions by empowering female business founders. "As a startup lab for women, we speak the same language, have common experiences. Having female founders together approaching a business in the way that matters to women creates a lot more confidence about launching and growing a company." As mentioned earlier, the Startup Lab's approach is based on the Japanese *hito* philosophy, which stands for support and accountability. Women's Startup Lab accepts three to four batches a year, each with about nine startup founders. The one-year program starts with an intensive, two-week, live-in accelerator immersion and ends with a two-week stay focused on funding activities. The program offers "transformational" CEO coaching, 120 hours of startup evaluation and strategy sessions, customer leads and introductions, networking, connecting, VC pitching, lectures, and how-to workshops. The program activities are very much centered on the startup founder. As Ari summarizes: "Women's Startup Lab is all about founder performance, about you as the founder. Do you come across persuasively? What is your mission? What is your story? Is your presence charismatic or timid? Are you confident? What about your financial knowledge and management style? All of these are necessary founder skills and part of our program."

Accelerating platforms

I conclude my analysis in this chapter by looking at accelerators that primarily offer office or exhibition space and that mainly get their revenue from rent or memberships, but on top of that may offer services that help startups to grow. Prospect Silicon Valley operates a non-profit technology demonstration center that focuses on the commercialization of new urban technologies to build smart, sustainable cities. It supports 16 to 18 startup companies at a time through a variety of support mechanisms: work and lab space to develop and exhibit new urban technologies, stakeholder connections, corporate partnering, investor referrals, network events, and innovation showcasing. Doug Davenport refers to these companies as his "startup clients", and the employees within Prospect who work with clients as his "champions". "Our champions", Doug tells me, " are really working with our startup clients to help them connect to the right people, to the right networks and stakeholders, and help them to develop their project or help get them advice." Prospect's role is to activate the urban ecosystem that a startup company seeks to innovate and to assist the founder team with product development, refinement, partner development, and going-to-market strategy.

GSVlabs houses over 170 startups in its 72,000-square-foot campus facility. As mentioned previously, it focuses on five verticals: big data, sustainability, education technology, entertainment, and mobile. CEO Marlon Evans asserts that: "One of our competitive advantages is that, because we focus a little bit later-stage, the programming that we offer can be very much tailored to that growth phase. We have specific programming around the five key vertical areas, and then we have general programming that is designed to prepare companies for this next phase of growth. We sit down with each of the startup companies at the beginning of each month and say 'How can we be helpful to you, how about your milestones?'" GSVlabs employs about 18 staff people to support the 170 startups divided over the five verticals. Marlon is very enthusiastic about Pioneer Accelerator, an intensive three-month program on startup acceleration that GSVlabs recently co-designed with Google Launchpad. The program consists of a boot camp on product development and marketing within the Google ecosystem; remote learning sessions on market validation and growth strategies; skills workshops on pitch coaching, brand building, and customer traction; mentorship and progress tracking; investor intros; and a Demo Day for invite-only investors.

Runway is a technology hub that provides co-working space for entre-preneurs, corporate innovation services, and innovation events. Runway is not just about office space, as Matt Walters explains. "We have partners that specialize in e.g. IP law, sales tactics, public relations, or HR. We do meet-up groups on connected cars, FinTech, augmented reality. We host panel discussions with successful entrepreneurs; we do corporate introduc-tions." Matt emphasizes the importance of having a vivid co-working office culture: "We are a community because of our culture. I think about culture a lot. You really need to spend a lot of time creating a strong community culture and tend to it. If we feel our teams are not collaborating enough, we will organize special events like matchmaking, like introductions, like happy hours. We want to create a community where startups are helping each other and where we are engaging with the startups." Runway also offers a special accelerator program on EdTech, together with the Michelson 20MM Foundation. The four-month, cohort-based virtual program supports innovations that improve the access and affordability of higher education. The program consists of targeted content and feedback via phone/video meetings, web-based presentations, and online collaboration.[69]

Hacker Dojo markets itself as a tech hub in the South Bay that is one part working space, one part events venue, and one part maker space: "The place to launch a software startup or build a robot." It does not offer a structured curriculum or formalized accelerator program to startup classes; instead, it is primarily a place where like-minded people work and meet and sometimes hang out. But it also offers a wide range of events, lectures, BarCamps, parties, and hackathons. A random sample of event titles from Dojo's early 2017 agenda includes: 'PixelHacks'; 'Bay Area's First All-Female High School Hackathon'; 'Learn JavaScipt'; 'Self Driving Car Study Group'; 'Discussion of Patents/IP'; 'IBM HackNight', 'Eight-Week VR Development

Class & VR Boot Camp'; 'Coder Dojo Silicon Valley: Advanced Coding for Youth'. These events are organized by Hacker Dojo's members. As executive director Jun Wong states: "Members are part of our volunteer community. Most of our events are run by members. This way, the Dojo stays mean and lean. We're not a traditional accelerator." Hacker Dojo, which is open 24/7, is attached to its co-working culture. "We try to make this an open place, we don't have too many formal rules, we're open to feedback, we're flexible, we depend on volunteers. All this happens naturally."

RocketSpace is one of the most prominent Silicon Valley co-working platforms, with a large San Francisco campus and with new locations in England, China, and Australia as of 2017.[70] It enables multiple corporates and later-stage startups to collaborate in an ongoing innovation and growth platform. Besides its 24/7 co-working space portfolio, RocketSpace organizes accelerator programs around a number of industries: food & agriculture, logistics, mobility, insurance, healthcare, retail, telecom, and media. The core of the programs is about connecting startups with leading industry mentors, product validation through pilot testing with corporate partners, feedback sessions, and investor introductions. RocketSpace takes on two startup cohorts a year per industry, with six to ten startups per batch. It holds a wide variety of weekly workshops and seminars on marketing, social media, sales strategies, tax issues, and IPOs, to name a few, and monthly so-called Trend Talks with industry leaders and entrepreneurs. RocketSpace's main selling point as a co-working space and as an accelerator is, according to Duncan Logan, "Connections. Our big thing for our startup clients is access to capital, access to corporates, access to each other, and then education around that. One of the things RocketSpace does very well is connecting founder teams to the marketplace. So, we might have teams come here and part of their business model is using Facebook as a platform. Well, we have great connections into Facebook, we can get to some of their key people in a day."

Conclusion

General/low-touch accelerators share a number of characteristics in terms of their programs. They admit larger numbers of startup team applicants (after strict procedures), are organized in batches or cohorts, and have a broad scope of technologies they are interested in. Most of them take equity, and their programs typically concentrate on relatively short periods (three to four months or shorter) and lead up to a Demo Day where prototypes are pitched to investors. Plug and Play, 500 Startups, and the Alchemist Accelerator all fit into this accelerator category.

Although their scalability and growth philosophy is technology-agnostic, these general/low-touch accelerators may introduce technology 'verticals' covering more specific sectors such as mobile, finance, media, Internet of Things, and health. Plug and Play is a good example. These accelerators do not admit startup teams on a rolling basis but work with classes of teams that participate and graduate as a cohort. The programs that are offered are structured almost as a standard school curriculum, with a clear beginning and a clear end. They include milestones, time frames, working towards a marketable product prototype, getting traction and first customers, structured team-investors meetings, and even graduation ceremonies. Their focus on classes or cohorts is based on the philosophy that startup teams all face similar challenges and that working with peers who go through comparable new-venture cycles makes a great difference.

Specialized/high-touch (domain-specific and niche) accelerators have a different growth philosophy. They believe in active co-creation through a hands-on approach. Accelerator executives work closely with their startup teams. Such an intensive, individualized method of company building is only possible when a limited number of startups are admitted to an accelerator. Some of these accelerators that do not provide in-house office or lab space have introduced smart methods of remote education and mentoring. All of these specialized accelerators – whether profit or non-profit – focus on business model refinement, product technology development, marketing, traction, targeted customer and investor introductions, and team building. The main goal of both general/low-touch and specialized/high-tech accelerators is to bring startup companies to the next level of funding through the development of a marketable and scalable product. Marketability and scalability are the magic words in the accelerator dictionary.

Accelerating platforms – "office space plus" accelerators – focus on providing co-working and/or lab space but also offer customer and investor introductions and organize event programming including workshops, seminars, guest lectures, and in-house startup happy hours. Silicon Valley accelerating platforms are not to be compared with traditional shared office buildings, as is customary in Europe. These platforms are much more entrepreneurial because they offer services that help startups to accelerate and link them to strategic networks of investors and customers.

6   Accelerator Darlings, Challenges, and Future Plans

All accelerators have their showcases of startups they see as their greatest successes. In this chapter, I analyze these accelerator darlings and the reasons they were nominated by my respondents. What is their underlying definition of success? Is it mainly related to the funds raised by accelerator startups or their social impact as well? The other side of success is, of course, failure. Do my respondents see a pattern in why startups fail? Does it come down to team, product, or market? It will become clear from my analyses that there is a multitude of factors related to startup success or failure. Predicting startup performance is a poorly developed discipline, much to the chagrin of accelerator CEOs and investors. But it is clear that traction is indispensable for a startup to grow to the next level.

I next examine the greatest challenges that accelerator executives face – challenges they need to address, challenges that are returning issues, challenges that dominate their management agenda. The chapter ends with a grander view and even some speculation. I asked respondents to share their dreams for the accelerator they run. How does the future look for their accelerator and which changes to their program are they planning?

Success, failure, and showcases

I asked accelerator executives why some startups are successful whereas others fail and which startups that graduated from their accelerator they are particularly fond of. Let us first examine some of the general accelerators. Predicting startup success is a tricky business, according to Elizabeth Yin of 500 Startups. Her accelerator has invested in over 1,800 startups, "But the funny thing is you just never know how things will go. You don't really know until it's over either way." For her showcases, Elizabeth nominates a number of stellar startups that participated in 500 Startups' seed and accelerator program, most of them B2B: Twilio (pay-as-you-go cloud communications platform), Credit Karma (credit and financial management platform), and Intercom (business messaging services). Twilio went public (IPO) in 2016, while Credit Karma raised $368 million and Intercom $115 million.[71]

Picking early winners is a major challenge faced by accelerators. Investor math is a matter of continuous trial and error. Saeed Amidi of Plug and

Play admits: "We all make mistakes. I had the opportunity to invest in Airbnb but we backed out. We had the opportunity to invest in Facebook really early. But all in all, we have around 20 startups that are close to half a billion valuation." Among Saeed's showcases are Dropbox (a cloud storage service), Lending Club (a peer-to-peer lending marketplace), SoundHound (audio recognition), Prevedere (business performance forecasting), and NatureBox (a healthy snacks delivery service). The funds that have been raised by these showcase examples are impressive: Dropbox raised $607 million, SoundHound $75 million, Prevedere $9.5 million, and NatureBox $58.5 million, while LendingClub went public in 2014.[72]

Danielle D'Agostaro of the Alchemist Accelerator pinpoints what makes startups successful: "The companies that hustle. They know how to execute, they know what they need to get done, and they do it. They don't let hurdles slow them down. If they can't get it in the first way, they try a hundred other ways to do it. They persevere, they are determined, they want to make this happen. I would say the successful ones tend to be the ones that are the hustlers." While the Alchemist is too young to have any graduates that have gone public, there have been about 13 acquisitions. For example, Assemblage (a cloud-based collaboration platform) was acquired by Cisco. Other showcase examples include Oomnitza (IT asset management), which raised $2.6 million; MightyHive (data-driven marketing), which raised $2.8 million; and Rigetti (quantum supercomputing), which raised $3 million.[73] With regard to Alchemist startups that Danielle herself gets really excited about, she says: "Honestly: the ones that are just world-changing." One of them is Positron Dynamics, which develops anti-matter rockets that would power the fastest spacecraft ever created and could eventually enable interstellar travel. Thinking big in optima forma. Positron is funded by a consortium of visionary investors that includes Peter Thiel, Tim Draper, and Ravi Belani.

At BootUP, Marco ten Vaanholt recently looked into just how successful his startups have been: "I was asking myself how many startups did I have over the last two years since we have this building? Ninety-eight companies, of which about forty graduated. None of them has failed. They have raised over $280 million already, and that's not because of us only, but because of the plays of good JuJu: their current valuation is at $3.5 billion. That's great. That's an amazing statistic." Marco believes that their success is related to BootUP's family-style and connectivity-style approach on how it does business. "It's a really personal relationship that we are building. It's more focused on giving back and doing the right thing. It's not always focused on making the most money. So it goes back to the DNA of BootUP. furthering entrepreneurialism. It's the ecosystem at work." Among Marco's personal favorites is AppMachine (creating mobile business apps), a Dutch company that was accelerated by BootUP. "Within ten months, we showcased real results with real pipeline, with real revenue, and real value. AppMachine was invested at an enormous amount by one of the largest website hosting companies in the world."[74]

When asked whether he could observe a pattern in factors that cause a startup to fail, Prashant Shah of TiE LaunchPad, replies: "I think the question you're asking is the million-dollar question. The question is simple but the answer is not. It's not just team or market conditions. That's too easy. Failure is very hard to predict." LaunchPad's high-risk profile makes it susceptible to failure. "Our plan is that over the life of our fund, we will invest in 40-50 companies. Maybe five of them will be the ones that actually make the fund profitable. Because we invest in early-stage startups with teams that are really first-time entrepreneurs, we know that the risk profile is very high on the fund. We have done three batches now, and in every batch there is always one company that seems to move ahead of the rest of them."

Gary Coover of Samsung NEXT weighs the difference between what makes a startup a success or a failure: "A lot of it has to do with the founders. Experience, tenacity, and knowing how to de-risk the startup are important success dimensions. Failure is often a result of being unable to prioritize efforts, to focus on the wrong things, which reduces the ability to drive real customer traction." Samsung has acquired a number of startups via its in-residence accelerator program, of which Gary gives two showcase examples: Mapzen (an open-source mapping platform) and StickiBoard (a shared family dashboard).

Asking Brian Hoffman about his favorite StartX startups evokes an understandable reaction: "It is like asking parents what their dearest child is." It could be about the founder, the team, the company's mission, its financial performance. Brian gives three examples of successful StartX companies: Periscope (a live video streaming app), which was acquired by Twitter; Life360 (a GPS family locator and messaging app), which raised $73 million; and Lily (drone cameras), which raised $15 million.[75] These are highly visible consumer brands, but as Brian indicates, some of the really big tech Stanford innovations – for example in the medical sector – are contributions to deep science that do not become consumer market startups but will be part of high-end enterprise technology. They are successful in terms of their contribution to society but not in terms of their mass visibility.

Cindy Klein-Marmer of Butler Venture Accelerator of Babson College notes that it has had successful student startups in its portfolio. "We have undergraduate students who come in and they have run businesses in their high school, they make five figures basically. They are very excited because they are sitting there with 10, 20, 30,000 dollars in revenue. It's not a million in revenue, it's not $100,000 in revenue, but some have come pretty close." Cindy gives an example of a student who ran a webhosting business that he started when he was 13, which earned a few million in revenue. This business later became his side business when he decided to launch a startup creating a file-sharing platform.

Specialized profit and non-profit accelerators all share the belief that traction is decisive. Traction determines whether a startup is on the right path; it also reflects product-market fit and team performance. Sunil Bhargava of Tandem believes very strongly that "traction is the key to success. A good team generates traction, and traction makes a team stronger." Sunil estimates that at least six out of ten startups will fail. "A lot of companies fail because they don't get traction for a variety of reasons. Because the founder is not seeing things in the right way and sometimes it is just the wrong thesis. Companies may have a good team, may have a good product, but they aren't able to crack the traction problem." Although Tandem is a relatively recent accelerator and investment fund, Sunil is proud to point to some successes. ZumoDrive is a cloud-based file synchronization and storage service that came to power HP's recent CloudDrive technology. Tandem helped ZumoDrive to pivot its initial product strategy. BashGaming, the casual game maker for social and mobile platforms, is another example. GSN later bought BashGaming for about $165 million.[76] Tile, a Bluetooth item tracker, is a third successful example and was Tandem's first hardware company; it raised $34 million.[77]

The Fabric, another recent accelerator, has built up a number of companies of which VeloCloud is the most shining example. It is a B2B providing software-defined wide area networking (SD-WAN) that raised $49 million in two rounds, with Cisco as an investor.[78] Prem Talreja is proud of The Fabric's role in accelerating VeloCloud: "It was the first startup we did and became a home run, a market leader. They could achieve north of $500 million to $1 billion validation. It has turned into a rock star market leader, our poster child so to speak."

The Hive, the co-creation studio, has seen over twenty startups go through its program since late 2012, four of which have successfully exited. Kosei, a startup that specializes in recommendation systems, was acquired by Pinterest in 2015; Deep Forest Media, a programmatic mobile marketing company and demand-side platform (DSP), was sold to Rakuten Marketing in the same year; Jobr, which developed a mobile job search app, was acquired by Monster Worldwide in 2016; and Nurego, a business operations platform for industrial internet applications, was acquired in early 2017.[79] T.M. Ravi explains why he gets so much personal satisfaction from coaching startups: "We play with cutting-edge technology: building software robots that automate customer support and customer software. We are playing with augmented reality and virtual reality. We are working on the frontiers of how we will be living our life in the next 25 years. We are creating something from nothing, and seeing it blossom and succeed. (...) There is no other thrill that is as fulfilling. You personally made it happen and it wouldn't have happened without you."

Niche accelerators have their share of successes and failures. Tom Ferguson of Imagine H_2O, has an interesting view of what makes a startup stronger: storytelling. "The biggest lesson is the importance of storytelling. You have to tell your story as a startup. It's not just marketing visibility, it's about understanding and communicating exactly what your business is about. Your company narrative and the way you tell it is absolutely critical." Nimesh Modak, Imagine's director, adds that startup failure is often related to underestimating the business importance of knowing your customer, of unlocking the market, which directly links to the topic of storytelling: "The better you know your customer, the better you know which story you need to tell." Three startup graduates Tom and Nimesh are particularly proud of are Valor Water Analytics, which transforms water utility data flows worldwide into actionable decision-making through innovative software; Nexus e-Water, which develops B2B water recycling hardware; and WaterSmart Software, which uses mobile and online tools to help water utilities educate and engage their customers to save water and money. These three Imagine H_2O darlings reflect a breadth of hardware and software technology in different water sectors. Valor Water Analytics was able to raise $2.8 million, Nexus-eWater $4 million, and WaterSmart Software $13.3 million in funding.[80]

Cleantech Open accelerates quite a number of startup companies throughout the U.S. Ian Foraker names two companies that rank high among his personal favorites. One is PowWow Energy – Cleantech Open 2013 winner – which provides Software as a Service (SaaS) solutions for increasing water use efficiency in the agricultural sector. It raised over $3 million in funding, including a grant from the California Energy Commission.[81] Ian: "One of the things they do is using the power signature of electric pump systems to tell whether there are leaks in agricultural fields. Fascinating technology, excellent founding team, great traction." The other favorite is Vartega – winner of the Cleantech Open 2015 national emerging technology prize – which specializes in carbon fiber-reinforced recycled plastic for mass use applications. "This has real significant implications for the growth of the whole recycling industry", Ian claims. Vartega raised $57,600 in equity funding and $250,000 in grants.[82]

Powerhouse CEO Emily Kirsch selects her five showcase examples based on a variety of reasons: innovation, mission, funding, traction, and diversity. Mosaic, which provides residential solar loans and financing, was what inspired the creation of Powerhouse and recently managed to raise $200 million in loan capital.[83] Powerhive is another of Emily's favorites because it supplies affordable micro-grid electricity for rural homes and businesses in developing countries around the globe, having first launched in Tanzania. PVComplete is a B2B platform for automating solar system design, and UtilityAPI provides instant access to utility bill data that can be used for solar company quotes. Both startups have substantial traction and were able to receive funding from the U.S. Department of Energy along with private capital (UtilityAPI raised $972,000).[84] And finally, Sunswarm is a community shared solar farm marketplace that Emily is especially proud of because it was one of the first movers in a huge market. Diversity is also key for Powerhouse: PVComplete and UtilityAPI have female co-founders and CEOs, and Sunswarm has an African-American founder and CEO. "At Powerhouse, it is important that not just our employees but also our founder teams reflect the diversity of our city [Oakland]." Empowering female startup founders and diversity is a major concern of Emily: "Because the bottom line for any company increases when women serve on boards in leadership positions. Less than four percent of U.S. venture capital goes to women, which is pathetic. What's even more pathetic is that one percent of venture capital funding goes to African-Americans and Latinos."[85]

Empowering female startup founders is the core business of Women's Startup Lab. Ari Horie notices that, after completing her accelerator program, founders gain a new level of confidence, have better networks, receive referrals, have access to funders, and have the right mindset and skills to be successful. Red Clay, a platform that connects brands to freelance industrial designers to turn product ideas into manufacture-ready technical files, has a prominent place in Women's Startup Lab's showcases. "We helped the founder with introductions to the circuit, and all those people were like, wow, she's great. She got a lot of attention, referral after referral, and she just took off." Red Clay raised $1 million in equity funding.[86] Another success story is Babierge, a platform that connects travelers with baby gear rentals (for example in airports), which has expanded to almost 90 locations in the

U.S. and Canada. In this case, too, the founder's increased confidence and network introductions made the difference.

I conclude this section by evaluating the five accelerating platforms. Prospect SV is a young innovation hub and demonstration platform launched in 2014. Founder Doug Davenport nominates ConnectMyEV, which provides smart and hands-free conductive chargers for electric vehicles, as one of Prospect's showcases. "This startup client is developing prototypes and is working with one of the largest car companies in the world. It's very, very interesting stuff." Thomas Power is another case. It works on retrofitting transit diesel busses in their mid-life stage by sustainable energy software and power management systems that transform them into hybrid and electric means of transportation. Doug reveals that the founder "is a really smart person who's got incredible experience and is leading a team in three countries. This startup client has gotten a couple of investment rounds and is starting on multi-million-dollar pilot projects."

Established in 2012, GSVlabs does not have a long track record, but Marlon Evans tells me that a few companies have already done very well. "A good example is an Australian company, LIFX, that raised over $15 million. We just had another company acquired by WeWork. More of those stories will be coming up, as we are still a young company." LIFX distributes Wi-Fi enabled, multi-colored LED lights controllable via a smart device.

When asked about his favorite successful startups, Runway's Matt Walters does not need to think long. One is Atomwise, which develops artificial intelligence systems for drug discovery: it raised $6.3 million.[87] "This is really cutting-edge data modeling using super computers and deep learning to simulate the effects of drugs from a compound of thousands of approved medicines that might, for instance, cure Ebola or MS. They partner with Merck, one of the largest pharmaceutical companies in the world." His second pick is Skycatch, which develops drones to analyze the progress at large construction industry sites delivering precision aerial mapping and 3D models. It managed to raise over $41 million.[88] "This, too, is fascinating technology. These drones are fully autonomous and self-charging, so they provide 24-hours continuous coverage." Skycatch partners with Komatsu, the world's second-largest construction equipment manufacturer.

Hacker Dojo's Jun Wong has a two-part answer to my question on the successful startups that came out of the Dojo. "What would the definition be? Well, I'll answer it the easy way and the hard way. In terms of market valuation, Pinterest is one of our showcases. But there are much smaller ones that launched good projects, creative projects, projects with an impact. We had a group here that was able to make a self-driving robot which you can drive around, recognizes people, and knows how to navigate. They were able to make this prototype out of $500 worth of material." Pinterest, the popular visual bookmarking tool for saving and discovering creative ideas, is in a different league: it raised total equity funding of $1.3 billion and is currently valued at $11 billion.[89]

RocketSpace's founder and CEO Duncan Logan attributes the success of his accelerator to its competitiveness, its infectious environment, and its entrepreneurial drive, in addition to the rigorous selection process. "This is Real Madrid [one of the most successful professional soccer clubs in Europe]." As a consequence, Duncan adds, "We've had an incredibly low failure rate. Of the 750 or so startup companies that have been through RocketSpace, the failure rate is about 15%." Uber, Spotify, and Zappos are among RocketSpace's famed alumni that went on to disrupt traditional markets and have a tremendous impact on consumer behavior.

To summarize, financial performance is a major element of how accelerator executives evaluate their startups' track record, particularly in terms of the amount of funding raised, whether or not they were acquired by a larger company, and whether they went public. Traction appears to be a determining factor in whether a startup will be successful or end in failure. Traction makes or breaks a startup. But this is not the whole story: innovation impact, social leverage, and market disruption were also named as important aspects of startup success. Many of the favorites chosen by accelerator executives succeeded in valorizing fascinating applications of breakthrough technologies.

Challenges and future plans

In this section, I examine some of the challenges that accelerator executives face and the business dreams they have for the near future. What strategic issues do they feel they need to address, and what innovations do they want to implement? Do accelerator founders and CEOs see a need for pivoting their business strategy?

At Plug and Play, one of the challenges and future plan is further expansion at both the national and international levels. CEO Saeed Amidi elucidates: "I want to have an innovation platform and accelerator on top of it. We just opened accelerators in China, Paris, Stuttgart, Berlin, and Amsterdam, and we may do New York City, London, and others in the future. Accelerators provide incredible opportunity for people to meet. They might be corporations from an industry that is being disrupted, or they might be from the venture world that is looking for investments." This expansion strategy is part of a larger scheme that Saeed dreams of realizing – a dream that consists of numbers and impact – personal impact, to be precise. "I have made a positive impact in about 6,000 startups since I opened Plug and Play. As I said, we recently opened new offices in China and Europe. My dream is that I would love to make a positive impact in like 10,000 startups; a 1,000 new ventures per Plug and Play vertical, and really change the industry. Half of it U.S., and half international. And then with all the startups in Germany, France, Spain, China, etc. we build a bridge to the mothership here in Silicon Valley. Their engineering teams could stay in Europe or Asia, but they have their headquarters here. That gives them access to the $6 billion to $10 billion market cap in the Valley."

Elizabeth Yin of 500 Startups has no grand plans for her accelerator but underlines that the accelerating startup program itself is a dynamic one. "It's a different program than it was a few years ago. And I fully expect that in another few years it will change again. I would love to grow our batches. But at this moment we are not anticipating building any accelerators outside the Bay Area. We may just increase the size of our batches." And what about 500 Startups' international ambitions? "Half of our investment partners are located outside of the U.S.: Europe, Asia, Middle East, Latin America. They help us with scouting startup companies and bring them here for the program. For fundraising, for the ecosystem, Silicon Valley remains one of the best places in the world. It makes sense to be here."

One of the challenges faced by accelerators that do not require mandatory program attendance is the danger of community erosion, of not building a strong startup batch culture. Danielle D'Agostaro of Alchemist Accelerator recognizes this challenge. "We need a balance. That's why we also have social events outside of just the educational components as well. There definitely is a stronger community between the people that show up regularly. We are also a little bit more open towards live streaming of our expert talks and founder presentations than we were before. It's a balancing act." But the majority does participate. They pay for the program, and many international founders move all the way out to Silicon Valley in order to attend the program. International expansion is on Alchemist's agenda. "We are actually in talks right now with some people who want to take Alchemist internationally, and we are looking at possible locations. I think in three years, Alchemist is not only going to be a Silicon Valley accelerator, and it's probably going to have its brand expanded, and not just in Europe."

Founders Space is a general but smaller accelerator. It has an international outreach but doesn't plan to turn the company into a mammoth accelerator. Naomi Kokubo says: "We've had investors requesting to invest in Founders Space. But we said no. We don't need the outside investment. But we are interested in setting up a good institutional venture fund not investing in us but in our startups." Founders Space would prefer to organize its international ambitions by using different templates, for example by franchising its model. "Having cobranded accelerators in China, Europe, Middle East, Asia, South America, and other parts of the world, with their independent organization and staff – this approach works very well." In May 2017, Founders Space announced that it was opening a branch in Chengdu, with other Chinese cities to follow.

TiE LaunchPad is also a smaller accelerator. Prashant Shah points to a challenge that is size-related. "Because we are so highly selective, the challenge is whether our present number of startups of about ten companies a year is sufficient to keep the program going. If we are only investing in a handful of startups, then the returns get longer as well. We are at a slower investment pace than most other venture funds, and that means that we have to start raising our next fund pretty early on." Does this self-diagnosis imply a pivot of the LaunchPad's main strategy? "Well, maybe. A solution might be that we have to invest in startups directly, even if they are not part of our program. See ourselves as angels." And in fact that is what LaunchPad recently decided to do: to continue as TiE Angels.

BootUP's Marco ten Vaanholt is passionate about the strength of Silicon Valley's ecosystem but also sees a serious challenge. "The climate here is that we have so many accelerators, everybody takes an equity position in early-stage startups between five and eight percent for 50-100K. That is a lot of money for a startup to give away– a lot of money for what is sometimes not more than a three-month pitch training. And then send them out into the world with $50,000. That's the downside." It is a model, according to Marco, that no serial startup entrepreneur is willing to accept. "What startups need is traction. And in traction they are willing to give up retainer fees, to give up revenue share, and only then they are willing to give up equity. Traction before funding, not the other way around. No funding before traction." This is just one step to Marco's dream for the future. "I want BootUP to become the de facto 'tractionator' of the world. I get the better startups with better survival prospects. I find it ridiculous that such a small percentage of startups succeeds." Part of Marco's dream is to work with European corporate partners and accelerate their startups in Silicon Valley. "BootUP built the ecosystem for doing so."

Does a corporate accelerator such as Samsung NEXT encounter different challenges than non-corporates? Yes and no, according to Gary Coover.

"We want to make sure that we are leveraging the strengths without also suffering from the perceived weaknesses of a large corporate." Competition for talent is a shared challenge. "There is definitely competition for talent. It's hard for good startups to hire great engineers, and it's hard for great accelerators to attract great talent. As a result, we think a lot about how we compete, how we can be different."

Cyril Ebersweiler, founder and managing director of HAX, raises a completely different challenge: what exit strategy will accelerators develop for themselves, not just for the startups they help grow? "What we soon will see is actual liquidity coming out of accelerators. They are creating enormous value for themselves. I think that accelerators will either be bought or they will go IPO. This really will change the playing field." If Cyril's prediction would become reality, it would certainly affect the way accelerators operate, their business model, the startups they seek to grow, their investment strategy, and the ROI they are after. It would impact the business parameters of accelerators in the future. What about HAX's own future? What are Cyril's dreams with respect to his own accelerator? "I would like to take on bigger projects. One is about building a new city. It is a ten-year program, but there are ways to do that. HAX Infra will play a major role. In three years, Infra will have a hundred companies that have the potential to implement a hundred technologies at the city level. I don't even know how to define it, but it is going to be fascinating. It's going to be big."

What are the challenges that university-linked accelerators encounter, and what are their plans for the future? StartX wants to rethink its business model. Says Brian Hoffman: "Our business model has some constraints in that we are limited in the number of our partners we can take because we are limited in the number of startups, we have a ten-week calendar. The assets that we have to provide to our partners do get diluted if we increase their number." This scaling issue is somewhat typical for a non-profit accelerator, Brian states. "When we started in 2010, we had a batch of eight companies, everyone was under twenty-five, doing it for the first time, and lived right around here. It's easy to build a community in a small ecosystem where people have so much in common. But as we grew we needed to professionalize, set up an organization, hire staff, be relevant to everyone." One of the challenges StartX as a general accelerator is facing is the issue of specialization, of finding the right balance between scaling, added value, and support quality. "We don't have to have that specialist value because we are a kind of lifelong Stanford network you can leverage, but we do need to have added value to every type of founder. How do you launch verticals, how can you be relevant to super specialized PhD teams?"

The Butler Venture Program of Babson College is a dynamic enterprise. "We are constantly changing" says Cindy Klein-Marmer. "I look at the accelerator as our startup, with me and my team members as founders. We are continuously tweaking and taking lessons on; there are constant iterations. This fall, we will roll out a new level of accountability and community." Cindy tells me that the San Francisco summer venture pilot, which they first ran in 2016, will be evaluated. Should it be made permanent? Could it be done remotely? Does it need to be on the West Coast? Does it need to be in the U.S.? These are all questions that come up for an accelerator as a learning enterprise, as a startup indeed. The Babson Venture Program also has international ambitions. "Through our new Babson collaborative, we are looking for a way to have additional accelerators and incubators, essentially around the world, based on a pay-to-play model. The opportunities are endless right now. It also makes sense with Babson's centennial anniversary coming up in 2019."

The specialized high-touch accelerators, including the smaller niche players, have their own concerns. Tandem, the hands-on mobile accelerator, understands that timing is everything. Sunil Bhargava has a clear view on Tandem's main challenge, one that holds for all quality-conscious accelerators: "I think the key challenge is finding the right team at the right moment. If the right team approaches us too late, it doesn't fit our model. If they approach us too early, it doesn't work either." For the future, Tandem is ambitious. Sunil: "My goal, you know, is more of a mission: to help out entrepreneurship on a global level. We want to do more startups that come from different parts of the world, help them build their company, and connect them to U.S. markets. The mission is having an impact on as many entrepreneurs as we can get through."

Prem Talreja of The Fabric defines a set of more practical challenges. "We decided that once we commit funding, we have to work with more stringent milestones. Funding is not a gift but needs timely accomplishments." The recruitment of founders also raises concerns, particularly with respect to mindset and expectations. "We have felt that people left their cushy jobs to come to us with the dream of becoming somebody that they were not ready for. There is a sense of comfort that they expect from a life as a startup entrepreneur, a life that actually is very uncomfortable – lots of stress, financial concerns, impact on your family and personal life. I've been there; I know what I am talking about." Managing growth is another issue that The Fabric is working on: "We have to focus more on ensuring the startups get future rounds of funding. Their success will help us refill our fund. Our intention is not to become a large organization. It would mean we have to expand our management team, solve lots of managerial problems. We are not like that."

At The Hive, T.M. Ravi's plans for the future reflect an energetic mix of passion, ambition, and impact: "Continue to create and launch exciting companies, help make their dream and the vision around artificial intelligence and its market potential become real – so real that it changes our lives – and see our startups go to greater and greater stages of success." The Hive's main focus is in Silicon Valley, but as part of its international expansion it has created The Hive India and The Hive Brazil. "We have sort of put The Hive in a box and made it easily transferrable to other regions. Some regions just don't have the innovation ecosystem, the capital, or the talent pool, so I wouldn't say it expands to everywhere but to some regions it definitely is. We are exploring some of them."

What are specific challenges that the four niche accelerators encounter? What about their plans for the future? Cleantech Open is a pro bono volunteer organization, which it believes is a major asset but also one that demands further professionalization. A volunteer organization typically faces challenges in the areas of structured coordination, less fluid participation, the creation of consistency and continuity, and the securing of institutional memory. In the words of Ian Foraker: "I think our core model is good, but it can be refined. We're always looking at ways we can make it more robust and leverage the asset we have. I'm eager to professionalize our model. We want to further standardize our main processes." One of these challenges has to do with fine-tuning Cleantech Open's admissions policy. "We are a mission-driven organization and therefore we want take as many viable startup companies in our accelerator program as possible. We have no shortage of mentors. In fact, we have mentor pools we can't leverage enough." The mission of Cleantech Open is to advance the use of sustainable resources and market-smart solutions to pressing environmental and energy issues. Ian states that the task for the near future is to create more value in realizing this commitment. "We need to move from being a passive catalyst to becoming an active catalyst. How do we not only educate entrepreneurs but actively evaluate the gaps and plug those gaps. We really want to expand our global footprint by connecting the dots across the globe. If we want to effectively fight global warming and climate change, we need to increase the bringing to market of innovative clean technologies by a factor ten or more."

For Imagine H_2O, "The challenge number one is to blow the minds of the entrepreneurs that take our program. We want them to be successful and our best evangelists possible." Having made this statement, Tom Ferguson points to a number of practical issues such as finding the right balance between training entrepreneurs and working remotely, and developing metrics to monitor the effectiveness of their programs. In terms of the future, Imagine H_2O's ambitions include further globalization. Nimesh Modak explains: "We want to explore how we can support startup companies from around the world. So much of the value we offer is through our mentorship program. In order to support startups in other countries, we need to expand our mentor and partner network. That is something we are quite aggressively pushing forward right now. It would really capitalize on the values of Imagine H_2O being a vertical accelerator."

In the solar energy industry, Emily Kirsch of Powerhouse reckons that "the biggest challenge is that not enough people are applying their skills to the solar industry yet. Eventually solar will be everywhere, it will power all of our lives, it will be built into our clothes, iPhone, and laptop covers, powering our homes and cars. This will all happen through innovative ways to produce and manage the distribution and storage of energy. And it all requires hightech and funding." Her greatest worry is that in spite of the enormous opportunity that solar presents and how big it is going to be in the near future, we are going to need much more talent and many more solar startup entrepreneurs. In the U.S., Emily discloses, there are 40 million rooftops that are suitable for solar, which would expand to 90 million households if apartments and condos are included. "We've only just begun scratching a tiny, tiny bit of the surface of what is possible." Emily predicts a bright future for community solar farms. "It's even going to be bigger than rooftop solar." Entrepreneurial talents and talented entrepreneurs are needed to make this radical energy transformation.

Ari Horie of niche accelerator Women's Startup Lab tells me that her organization is expanding with a venture division and a co-working division. She's moving the startup lab "beyond" the core business of an accelerator, thereby moving to a new stage of her lab's story with much more emphasis on lifelong education and platforms for women entrepreneurs. The new program will focus on batches of "the nine best and brightest female entrepreneurs". In Chinese numerology, the number nine has a very positive connotation and stands for luck, creativity, imagination, dream realization, and care. Ari's dream is to set up the new model in a way that is scalable and that makes Women's Startup Lab into a global entrepreneurship brand podium that supports female entrepreneurs in launching and growing their companies. She aims for it to be a model that helps women to thrive and succeed, where meaningful relationships and new technology bring unlimited opportunity.

And what are the challenges and future plans of the five accelerator platforms that feature in my study? Prospect SV is an innovation hub and demonstration center that works with corporate sector players, innovative startups, cities, agencies, and the research community – a complex field of stakeholders according to Doug Davenport. The challenge? "It's just incredibly hard to actually make that become a symphony, right? We could teach classes on this. At the end of the day, you need momentum. The problem is that the market isn't moving fast enough for there to be any pull of ideas in." Prospect helps Bay Area cities in becoming smart and sustainable communities. "The biggest problem is that 108 cities in the Bay Area are not acting as a 108 division region. They're all individual, independent entities, sometimes at cross purposes with each other. Our biggest challenge here is to help build the business case in those cities." Doug's ideas for the future are directly related to addressing these challenges. One is to help elevate innovation leadership and early technology adoption amongst certain cities and develop cases that other cities can learn from. "That would be fantastic." The other is to promote capability development among industrial stakeholders – e.g., the building industry – to help them understand how they can benefit from new technologies. "Such a focus on design feedback and market intelligence could make a unique program."

One of the challenges that Marlon Evans of GSVlabs shares is determining the basics of his accelerator's expansion model. Which new domestic and international markets are suitable? How do you get there? What are the business model implications, and what funding do you need? "If you look at a market like China, I think there are like 10,000 accelerators, probably a new accelerator a day that's starting up. How do we play in that environment, and does it make sense to start a new accelerator or do we service as a hub that these other accelerators can use as a resource"? GSVlabs' model will change as markets develop, says Marlon, "but the core will always be working with startups. The value added that we could provide is going to be more of a platform ecosystem where ideally we support accelerators that move into new markets. A kind of retail model. A kind of scaling model."

Runway is also re-examining its business model. At present, it combines co-working incubation space with a specialized EdTech accelerator. Matt Walters sketches the challenges and ambitions: "We are considering doing additional acceleration programs in other fields. We are debating whether this makes sense, or could we instead just have our incubator and then have a fund and invest in the startup companies without having to run additional programs." A more practical challenge is for Runway to track more metrics on how their startup companies are doing: monitoring traction, investments, funding, etc. "We want to be more analytic-driven, we want to measure impact." Like GSVlabs' Marlon Evans, Matt points to the rapidly growing number of accelerators. "Every week I hear about another one popping up. The challenge for us is to make sure that we are continuing to deliver value, that we really provide the services and resources out there." And as with other accelerators, Runway has global ambitions: "The dream is to have Runway locations around the world. So we are going out to South America, we are going out to East Asia to create a global network. I think there is something powerful about being able to connect different geographies."

The biggest challenge for Hacker Dojo, according to Jun Wong, is real estate. "Because we are non-profit, we want the Dojo to be accessible to everyone. But there is a huge cost in operating this place as rents get higher and higher." What is also high is Hacker Dojo's ambition. "We're trying to raise a really big fund so that we can purchase a campus. That's our goal for the next three years." Hacker Dojo furthermore wants to refine and expand its open model of self-education. "We would like to have a broader approach in which our members can learn from others by bringing in people that are leaders in their field and discuss and share their experiences. That would be a very 'Dojo-esque' kind of thing."

RocketSpace intends to go global, as Duncan Logan explains: "We've been working a lot on this. We started here in Silicon Valley because it's a kind of mecca for technology, but I think there are ecosystems elsewhere around the world that would work for us. We might put a RocketSpace in London or Amsterdam, Berlin or Tel Aviv, or Singapore or Shanghai. And we just focus on the top 200 companies and then we connect them together." In April 2017, RocketSpace opened its first European co-working campus in London.[90]

Conclusion

The success or failure of a startup is hard if not impossible to predict, according to Silicon Valley accelerator executives. Forecasting a startup's success is more intuitive than hard science. Predicting startup success is a Herculean undertaking. But in every scenario traction is key. Customer traction is the conditio sine qua non for startup growth. Scalability is essential. The startups that respondents selected as their showcases are the ones that raised considerable external funding, which is, of course, traction-related. The products or services launched by these favorites are believed to have a significant social impact as well. Accelerator founders and CEOs are intrigued by cutting-edge technologies that address urgent short or long-term issues and that develop solutions that disrupt markets. Most of them are market and mission-driven. Scalability and market prospect is what defines startup potential, and to develop this potential requires experience, tenacity, and team prioritizing. But even then, there is no single path to success. What are some of the most common mistakes founder teams make in this context? Seasoned mentor and Silicon Valley connoisseur Susan Lucas-Conwell does not have to think long: "The most deadly one is when the team is solving a problem that nobody cares about. The next one is that the team works on a solution that nobody wants to pay for."

One challenge was mentioned by nearly all my respondents: talent. All accelerators are looking for talented startup teams. Regardless of sector, mission, profit or non-profit status, size or program, an accelerator's primary concern is getting access to talent and recruiting talented startup founders. Accelerator executives feel that they are all competing for the best startup teams. Additional challenges include specialization, further professionalization, increasing cohort size, stakeholder alignment, and the need for monitoring startup performance by using more advanced metrics.

High tech is essentially global: it is not restricted to geographical markets, boundaries, or national entities. It is interesting that so many Silicon Valley accelerators indicate that going global is among their priorities in the near future. Most accelerators have international ambitions and want to expand to other regions and countries. 'Global branding', 'global franchising', 'global outreach', 'global connectivity', and 'global platform and hub' are expressions the accelerator executives use to illustrate their international aspirations. The typical global strategy of accelerators has been to train international startup teams in Silicon Valley. Now they see that other countries and regions are becoming interested in developing innovative ecosystems as well. This leads to a reverse strategy in which accelerator branches are to set up in other parts of the world. The underlying dream is not only based on broadening their geo-economic investment calculus but also inspired by a deeper mission of having a global impact on fostering entrepreneurship.

7   What Can Europe Learn From Silicon Valley Accelerators?

Accelerators can greatly contribute to advancing a dynamic European startup economy. This study has examined 23 accelerators in Silicon Valley with the aim of inferring some lessons on how to create a stronger and more vibrant startup community in Europe. In addition to presenting the main conclusions of my study, I outline ten practical decision rules for aspiring European accelerators that I believe will ensure their effectiveness. These ten rules are based on my chief findings from this study. I conclude the book by sharing some thoughts on the substantial role that accelerators can play in boosting Europe's startup economy.

Main findings and lessons

Silicon Valley's remarkable track record as a global innovation and startup hotspot never ceases to amaze the rest of the world. The region has become a paragon for policymakers, innovation stakeholders, ambitious entrepreneurs, and hungry startup founders. Its track record is based on a consistent and resilient ecosystem that secures access to talent, venture capital, support facilities, and a willing government. Its performance is driven by a culture that stimulates big thinking, sharing, competition, and risk-taking. Silicon Valley has launched startups that grew into companies that have changed our way of communicating, our lifestyle, and even the world. Apple, Google, Facebook, Twitter, WhatsApp, Instagram, Uber, and Airbnb are prominent examples. But it is also a region where there is significant inequality between insiders and outsiders, between high-tech *nouveau riches* and underprivileged social groups. For many members of the lower and middle class, Silicon Valley is no longer a place they can afford to live in. This is the painful downside of the Valley's success story.

During the last five to ten years, Silicon Valley has witnessed a rapid increase in accelerators helping startups to develop and grow their business. These 'schools of startup entrepreneurship' assist new ventures to sharpen their business concept, to calibrate their business model, to get first customers and traction, to pitch to angel investors and VCs, and, most importantly, to scale their venture. Silicon Valley's math is all about fast growth. In this study, I attempt to understand the role that accelerators play in taking startups to the marketplace, in expanding their market impact, in helping them to get traction and to scale up, and in bringing them to the next round of funding. I do so in the hope that European countries can learn from the Silicon Valley accelerator phenomenon in order to bridge the entrepreneurial divide and innovation gap between Europe and the U.S.

I interviewed 23 accelerators from all over Silicon Valley, which provided me with considerable insight into how these 'growth engines' operate and how they approach the puzzle of accelerating the life cycle of innovative startups. More specifically, I looked at accelerators' mission and philosophy, technology focus and target group, business model, admittance procedures, cooperation networks, program content, and mentoring as well as the main challenges they face and their plans for the future.

Accelerators are in great demand among startup founder teams, as the latter understand that participation in these growth programs will improve their market opportunity and investment chances. Accelerators, in turn, are highly selective in admitting startups. Only the best and brightest teams are accepted, based on stringent selection procedures. The right combination of team, technology, and market is paramount. In general, Silicon Valley accelerators do not admit solo founders because the risk of failure is simply too high. Running a startup is extremely demanding and requires multiple skills and competences that are seldom incorporated in one single person. Running an accelerator is equally demanding and in many cases resembles launching and growing a startup, with all the complexities and struggles it takes.

Accelerators in Silicon Valley vary significantly in terms of key features such as mission, business model, size, program structure, and mentoring. I observed a chief dichotomy between general/low-touch accelerators and specialized/high-touch (domain-specific and niche) accelerators. This distinction turned out to be very helpful in explaining the differences between accelerators.

On one side of the continuum, we have large general accelerators that do not focus on one specific technology or target group but accept startups across a broad spectrum of technologies. To add substance, accelerators may introduce so-called 'verticals' (single technologies), e.g., health, mobility, robotics. These accelerators are primarily interested in volume, i.e., in preparing large numbers of startups for commercial take-off. Their investment logic is based on the assumption that a few successful startups will raise significant accelerator revenue that will make up for the losses of most others. These accelerators tend to have strong links with the VC community. Accelerators typically offer short, standardized growth programs (three to four months) to several startup classes a year. Mentoring is part of the program but on a low-intensity basis (low-touch). The program usually culminates in a demo day where startups will present their prototypes to investors. Taking equity is a common investment policy among these accelerators. In many cases they operate as investment vehicles: their business model is to find startups that will be mega-successful – the "next big thing". For many outside observers, these general/low-touch accelerators represent the mainstream accelerators. Well-known examples are Plug and Play and 500 Startups.

On the other side of the continuum, we find specialized/high-touch accelerators. These are smaller accelerators that focus on bringing a limited number of startups to the market. They concentrate on particular technologies (for example artificial intelligence, cloud infrastructure, mobile) or niche markets (solar, clean technology, water) and actively coach their startups in a very hands-on (high-touch) way. The startups are not organized into classes, as they are mostly accepted on a rolling basis. They are not provided with standardized growth programs, and the length of in-house coaching is not fixed. These accelerators' ROI strategy and equity policy depend on their mission: some specialized/high-touch accelerators are for-profit (e.g., The Hive, Powerhouse), while others are non-profits (Imagine H$_2$O, CleanTech, and Women's Startup Lab).

It should be noted that this differentiation between the two accelerator types does not necessarily correspond to the distinction between commercial and mission-driven accelerators. Though most general/low-touch accelerators are for-profit companies, there is a mixed pattern among specialized/high-touch accelerators. And in any case, quite a number of for-profit accelerators are managed by highly content-driven executives who all share a passion for making an impact.

A third category of startup growth facilitators are accelerating platforms. They primarily offer office or lab space to startups, but they may also arrange access to VCs and provide elementary business support. They do not see themselves as investors but generally work together with the corporate world. These platforms offer startups a stimulating environment in which to grow. Examples include RocketSpace and Runway.

Accelerators also differ with respect to their market focus in terms of B2B or B2C, software or hardware. These choices obviously directly affect the way that accelerators are organized (selection, program, mentors, funding) and the resources they need (e.g., engineering expertise, hardware lab, suppliers). Hardware accelerator HAX differs completely from software accelerator TiE LaunchPad, even though both accelerators target enterprise-focused startups.

Mentoring startups is what all accelerators see as their core activity, either high-touch or low-touch. The Silicon Valley pool of mentors coaching accelerator startup teams is phenomenal. All the executives I interviewed stress that there is no shortage of committed and experienced mentors. This appears to be part of the Valley's culture of giving back. Mentors are often former entrepreneurs who want to share their expertise and networks and enjoy being involved in the valorization of new technologies. They give their counseling for free. But their motives are not per se purely altruistic, as they may have a personal interest in helping startups go to market. Access to gifted startup mentors is what makes an accelerator. In the specialized, smaller high-touch accelerators, startups are coached – on a day-to-day basis – by accelerator executives. A perfect mentor-startup fit is imperative.

Accelerators offer a range of programs for their startups, depending on their mission and focus. Program formulas differ in length, intensity, standardization, and coaching offered. Some programs are cohort-based (which is usually the case with larger general accelerators), while others are tailor-made (which tend to be seen at smaller, domain-specific and niche accelerators). But all programs and coaching activities share a core that is relevant to all startups. Founder teams need to develop their business idea, to figure out the growth and scalability options, work out their business model and company strategy, come up with a marketing plan, prepare themselves for go-to-market, get first customers and sales, pivot their product and strategy based on market responses, work out team issues, pitch to venture capitalists, and cope with the many practical issues that startups face. Accelerators help startup teams in addressing these issues and making their business stronger.

Silicon Valley accelerators excel in organizing events, reflecting their active involvement in the startup community. Workshops, lectures, speaker sessions, seminars, tutorials, roundtables, and founder team presentations are all part of the services that accelerators offer to their startups. All this adds to a vivid, inviting, and entrepreneurial accelerator culture.

All accelerator executives agree that predicting startup success is often more about intuition, hindsight, and lots of luck than about proven quantitative models. It's not just team, technology, or market that leads to success, but it is clear that having a malfunctioning team, weak technology, and no traction will more than likely lead to failure.

Accelerators work with outside partners, mostly on an informal basis, sometimes in a more structured way. Collaboration with investors is a top priority, as it gives them access to funding. And investors have a clear interest in being involved with accelerators: it brings them into contact with the most talented startups and promising new technologies. Accelerators also cooperate with other agencies within the Silicon Valley ecosystem: universities, innovation and industry stakeholders, and the corporate world. Lawyers are particular useful in giving legal and business advice to startup teams. They often work on the basis of deferred fees, meaning that startups will be charged when revenues come in and not earlier. This greatly helps startups in the early stages of the business cycle.

A trend can be observed in which large corporates start their own in-house accelerators. This keeps them in touch with innovative ideas and with new technology that can stimulate their business activities and market – maybe not today but probably tomorrow. Moreover, by bringing in startups into their labs and research centers, they can energize their innovation and entrepreneurial corporate culture. Samsung NEXT is an example of a corporate accelerator.

There were a number of similarities in the responses given by the interviewees regarding the challenges they face and their plans for the future. They all underline the importance of having a unique selling point that separates them from the competition, of getting the right startup teams at the right moment, of optimizing the number of startups, and of achieving a fair number of winners. Talent is probably the main concern cited by the accelerator executives. Mission-driven accelerators feel the permanent need to balance purpose and professionalization.

Interestingly, nearly all accelerators are involved in trajectories to internationalize their organizations and to reach out to other continents and countries. Some have very concrete plans, while others are still considering the modalities (e.g., franchising, new branches, co-branding, hubs). Pioneering Silicon Valley accelerators that have already entered the European market include Plug and Play and RocketSpace. Most Silicon Valley accelerators, it has to be stressed, are very international in that the startup teams they coach come from all over the world.

A final word on accelerator success: most accelerators in Silicon Valley are relatively young companies that lack a balanced and validated set of performance metrics. They tend to illustrate their success by pointing to the funds that 'their' portfolio startups have collectively raised after leaving the accelerator. This fundraising algebra – also known as 'vanity metrics' – may look quite impressive but needs some serious debunking. This especially holds true for the larger, general/low-touch accelerators. The main issue, naturally, is whether there is a causal relationship between accelerator participation and startup success. We need much stronger empirical evidence. Developing and reporting solid performance indicators should be a major priority for professional accelerators. This is particularly true given that new accelerators are popping up on an almost daily basis.

Bridging Europe's innovation gap

European policymakers agree that, in comparison to the United States, Europe is lagging behind in innovation, entrepreneurship, and new venture creation. Data indicate that the U.S. outperforms Europe in terms of R&D spending, the number of new businesses and first-time entrepreneurs, the available amount of venture capital, and the number of fast-growing companies (scale-ups). It also imposes less bureaucracy on startups (Entrepreneurship 2020; Ester & Maas 2016; European Investment Bank 2016; Horizon 2020). The nature of the entrepreneurial divide between both continents is rooted not only in institutional differences but also in cultural factors. Europe is more risk-averse, and entrepreneurial ambition is less applauded. For many Americans – certainly those living in Silicon Valley – successful startup founders and serial entrepreneurs are celebrated role models.

The U.S. ecosystem for startups, and in particular the Silicon Valley version, is more elaborate and balanced with respect to access to funding, talent, support networks, and government facilitation. It has a much longer tradition, too. What is equally relevant is that the system is grounded in a strong entrepreneurial spirit; its culture breathes risk-taking and excellence. I know that these conclusions sound rather general, but their truth is not disputed. Just think for a moment: would it have been possible for Google, Apple, Facebook, Uber, or Airbnb to have been European companies? In terms of ideas, maybe; in terms of commercialization, probably not.

European policymakers have become concerned about Europe's innovation gap: compared to the United States, the Old World is less adept at taking innovations to market. As Jyrki Kaitanen, European Commission Vice President for jobs, growth, investment and competitiveness, stated: "Europe has been good at turning Euros into knowledge, but not that good at turning the new knowledge into Euros and jobs."[91] There is a gap between inventiveness and marketability, between brilliant ideas and market response, between innovation and commercial implementation. American startups are much more focused on valorizing their innovations, on bridging the innovation gap – in simple terms, to make money out of innovation. As we have seen, all the incentives and parameters of the Silicon Valley ecosystem converge to help bring innovations to the market. Accelerators play a pivotal role in this

Some Silicon Valley gurus are quite gloomy about Europe's potential to turn the tide. Veteran technology investor and PayPal founder Peter Thiel is one of them. Though it has not prevented him from investing considerably in high-tech European startups, Thiel was brutally critical of Europe's lack of innovativeness and entrepreneurship in a 2014 interview with the Financial Times: "I think people in Europe are generally pessimistic about the future. They have low expectations, they're not working hard to change things. When you're a slacker with a pessimistic view of the future, you're likely to meet those expectations."[92]

In his book *Zero to one*, also published in 2014, Thiel typifies Europeans as "indefinite pessimists".[93] Coincidence or not, in the same year the European Commission launched *Horizon 2020*, the largest EU research and innovation program ever with nearly € 80 billion of funding available over seven years (2014 to 2020).

The main goal of *Horizon 2020* is to boost Europe's global innovativeness and competitiveness: "It promises more breakthroughs, discoveries, and world-firsts by taking great ideas from the lab to the market." (Horizon 2020: 1). This is a sentence that could have been penned in Silicon Valley. The program links research to innovation and is focused on excellent science, industrial leadership, and the tackling of major social issues. The program aims to re-establish Europe's position in producing world-class science and to remove unnecessary red tape that hinders innovation. Enabling funding for premier research is the key pillar of *Horizon 2020*. The areas covered include nanotechnologies, advanced materials, biotechnologies, IT, space, health, food, agriculture, forestry, energy, transport, and climate action. The number of proposals that were submitted under the program's first 100 calls was 36,732; 14% of which were retained for funding. *Horizon 2020* has turned into the main and largest European funder of research and innovation, with a strong emphasis on bridging the innovation gap. And, importantly, the market potential of innovations is a basic funding criterion.

Just prior to the Horizon program, the EC launched its *Entrepreneurship 2020 Action Plan*. The new initiative is based on the realization that in order "to bring Europe back to growth and create new jobs, we need more entrepreneurs." (Entrepreneurship 2020: 3). The idea is to "unleash" Europe's entrepreneurial potential, remove barriers, and accelerate its entrepreneurship culture. The program consists of three action pillars:

a)   Entrepreneurial education and training to support growth and business creation (increasing and improving practical entrepreneurial learning, especially within higher education);

b)   The creation of an environment in which entrepreneurs can flourish and grow (better access to finance, early-stage investors, and alternative funding; tax incentives; better use of ICT; easier business transfers; making bankruptcy less insuperable for second starters; simpler rules for startups; access to incubators and business accelerators);

c)   The development of role models in order to reach out to specific groups (entrepreneurship promotion; becoming an entrepreneur as a regular career choice; and stimulating startups among women, seniors, migrants, the unemployed, and young people).

Each of the three pillars is translated into a number of specific policy proposals and recommendations for the individual EU member states. It is one of the first EU documents that mentions the role of accelerators in building new ventures, albeit only briefly.

One further EU initiative needs to be mentioned that is allied to the Entrepreneurship 2020 program: *Startup Europe*.[94] Its main goal is to strengthen the European business environment for tech entrepreneurs by providing access to support services such as business advice, networking, and legal assistance. *Startup Europe* aims to inspire the business community, acknowledge role models, and celebrate new and innovative startups. It launched the Accelerator Assembly, which operates as Europe's prime network for startup accelerators.[95] The Assembly is an industry-led network to connect accelerators all over Europe and to act as "a forum delivered by the accelerator community, for the accelerator community." The forum shares information on key trends in the world of tech accelerators, exchanges best practices on startup growth programs, organizes meetings and conferences, and publishes guides to European accelerator programs. The target group is the leaders of accelerators that help founder teams to build and grow their business.

Until very recently, Europe was well behind the U.S. – and certainly behind Silicon Valley – in making the transition to a startup economy. But in the last few years, Europe has taken a leap forward, launching a number of programs designed to encourage entrepreneurship and fuel an entrepreneurial culture. Much still needs to be done, and it needs to be done in a way that is consistent with basic European values and social preferences. Europe must find its own way towards a flourishing startup economy; it cannot 'copy & paste' the Silicon Valley model. Individual European countries are working hard to build ecosystems that, with the help of accelerators, will become fertile environments for startups to blossom. Cities such as London, Berlin, Stockholm, Paris, Amsterdam, Barcelona, Madrid, and many others are becoming fine examples of energetic startup hubs.[96] The fact that Silicon Valley investors are actively investing in European startups is a case in point. But there still is a long way to go, if only because individual European countries differ markedly in their approach to addressing the innovation gap (Veugelers 2016) and implementing policies promoting entrepreneurship and startups. In the next section, I look at the startup climate in a European country I know best: the Netherlands.

The Netherlands: StartupDelta

In the last five to eight years, the startup scene in the Netherlands has developed rapidly and it is now turning into a mature economic community that fosters innovation and entrepreneurship. Launching viable startups is a high priority on the Dutch economic policy agenda. People in the Netherlands understand that startups add to the competitiveness of the Dutch economy, particularly if startups are able to make the transition to fast-growing scale-ups. Successful Dutch startups with a global significance include Ayden, WeTransfer, Booking.com, and TomTom. Some fast-growing runner-ups include Catawiki, Takeaway.com, Elastic, Gitlab, and Picnic.

There are a number of flourishing startup hubs in the Netherlands, particularly in the Eindhoven area (Philips High Tech Campus, ASML, NXP, FEI), the Rotterdam region (seaport-related innovation, logistics, and clean technology), the Wageningen area (food and agriculture), Delft University (engineering and hardware), and Amsterdam (the center of Dutch venture capital). The 2017 Global Startup Ecosystem Report lists Amsterdam in the top 20 of worldwide best-performing startup cities and habitats (Silicon Valley being number one). Only four other European cities rank higher: London, Berlin, Paris, and Stockholm.

In 2014, StartupDelta was launched to advance, coordinate, and promote the Dutch startup ecosystem. It was first led by Special Envoy and former EC Commissioner Neelie Kroes, followed in 2016 by Prince Constantijn of Orange-Nassau – the younger brother of the Dutch monarch Willem-Alexander – who is an acclaimed aficionado of startups and new technology. A publicly backed initiative, StartupDelta's aim is to make the Netherlands the best-connected and largest startup ecosystem in Europe. The initiative brings together the government, the corporate world, startups, universities and research labs, and investors. The mission according to Dutch Prime Minister Mark Rutte is the shared goal of "making the Netherlands an ideal location for startups, where young entrepreneurs with futuristic ideas can turn their dreams into reality."[97] StartupDelta has introduced startup visas for foreign startup founders, initiated a so-called corporate launch pad, and is involved in informing companies from abroad how they can grow their business in the Netherlands.[98] Recently, it convinced the Dutch government to introduce fiscal incentives to invest in startups and to lower startup labor costs.

Encouraging close collaboration between corporates and startups is a priority of StartupDelta. To further this goal, in 2016 the COSTA (COrporates and STArtups) program was launched by Special Envoy Neelie Kroes together with Jan Kees de Jager, CFO of KPN and former Dutch Minister of Finance. "The reasoning is that collaboration between nimble startups and corporates that have scale and leverage will accelerate the pace of innovation in the Netherlands."[99] As part of this long-term program, 19 Dutch corporate giants (including Shell, Philips, ASML, Unilever, Rabobank, KPN, AkzoNobel, and KLM) committed themselves to jointly enter partnerships with more than 300 startups within a period of less than one year.[100] The underlying idea of this major initiative was to boost the innovative power of the Netherlands, deepen its ecosystem, promote lasting cooperation between the corporate world and startups, and accelerate sustainable economic growth.

In 2017, StartupDelta introduced a new Action Plan that seeks to connect and promote the Dutch startup ecosystem as one single hub. It also published a Startup Manifesto with a number of policy priorities to make the Netherlands *the* startup country in Europe. The plan sets a number of objectives: to grow the overall pool of top-tier foreign venture capital and 'smart funding' by making the Dutch fiscal system more competitive internationally, to link Dutch startups to the rest of the world through trade missions and international hubs, to connect and improve national and international mentoring networks, to link startups and corporates, to legally allow for an online procedure for new ventures to start their businesses, to make education more entrepreneurial, to enlarge the talent pool, and to address the pressing shortage of tech talent. Proposed actions also emphasize the need for less stringent regulations on new technology, a more active role for the government as a launching customer for startups, a more flexible labor market to hire startup employees, and a system to challenge and reward universities for launching spin-outs and boosting startups. The Action Plan specifies the new goals as concretely as possible and includes targets for operational key performance indicators (KPIs).

The Action Plan and the Startup Manifesto's focus on attracting more foreign venture capital and on enlarging the startup talent pool is understandable. The latest Global Startup Ecosystem Report, mentioned above, indicated outstanding performance metrics (e.g., exit values) for the Amsterdam-StartupDelta, but as the Report concludes, "it could generally improve access to talent and funding" (2017: 76). But, it has to be added, it is not merely a case of re-adjusting the institutional parameters of the ecosystem. Culture also matters. The Netherlands could do a better job of growing new companies with a global impact. As Dutch startup ambassador Prince Constantijn makes clear: "We sometimes lack a sense of urgency. We need to fuel our entrepreneurial drive, the desire to be the best. At the same time, startups often feel they're left to fend for themselves. Their financing comes from venture capital funds in the U.S. People over there sometimes have a better idea of who's doing well here than we do!"[101]

Though StartupDelta is not an accelerator program, it prides itself in acting as a gateway to accelerators and other ecosystem facilitators in the Netherlands. The country has a number of reputed incubators and accelerators such as YES!Delft (2005), Rockstart (2012), Startupbootcamp (2010), whose growth programs incorporate many elements of their Silicon Valley role models, particularly with respect to startup selection, technology focus, team composition, program format, mentoring, access to investors, and corporate partnerships. For many new Dutch accelerators, top Silicon Valley accelerators are leading examples of how to execute startup growth programs.

Accelerator decision tool: Ten basic questions

Accelerators, as we have seen, come in all shapes and sizes. Though they all strive for startup development and growth, they are based on different philosophies, different investment strategies, and different business missions. Accelerators help startups to refine and scale their business proposition and to define their go-to-market options but do so in a variety of ways. Their growth programs differ in structure, technology focus, target group, size, recruitment, coaching, and mentoring. Accelerators, moreover, vary in terms of business model and equity policy. A differentiation that turned out to be instrumental in my study is the one between general/low-touch accelerators, specialized/high-touch accelerators, and accelerating platforms. This differentiation clearly reflects these different organizational parameters.

Based on my findings and analysis of the 23 Silicon Valley accelerators in this study, I have formulated ten basic questions that should facilitate entrepreneurs, innovation stakeholders, and policymakers in Europe and elsewhere intending to design and build an accelerator. This is a simple but fundamental decision tool that crystallizes the *raison d'être* of every accelerator wanting to coach, launch and grow successful startups. These guidelines are solidly grounded in the main findings of my research.

It should be noted that, by its nature, launching an accelerator does not fundamentally differ from launching a startup. As a consequence, most of the rules that apply to building a startup pertain to building an accelerator as well.

In the coming years, the number of new accelerators in Europe will most certainly increase rapidly. My hope is that the following decision tool will be instrumental in helping them set up their business in a professional and appealing way – one that takes into account the experience of Silicon Valley accelerators.

1. Mission: for-profit or non-profit?
    The first question is whether the accelerator's main goal is to make money or whether it is primarily mission-driven without the sole intention of being profitable. Some accelerators are first and foremost interested in growing startups that will generate handsome revenues, while others are inspired by the need to solve urgent social problems. The first objective implies recruiting startups that are high-growth traction potentials; the second objective leads to searching for startups that could have a major societal impact. It should be emphasized that in reality there is a gray area between these two opposite ends of the spectrum. But choosing one or the other of these two principal objectives will predetermine an accelerator's ROI strategy, startup selection process, stakeholder involvement, and equity policy – in short, its business model.

2. Focus: general or niche market?
    The next basic question to ask is whether the accelerator will take a technology-agnostic approach to growing innovative startups or whether it will focus on specific technologies (e.g., mobility, artificial intelligence, health) or niche markets. This choice directly affects an accelerator's recruitment process, coaching programs, investor profiling, and stakeholder participation. A tendency I observed among the larger Silicon Valley general accelerators was to include specific verticals that add to incremental specialization. Niche players tend to be smaller, though they can be larger in domains such as clean

technology. Smaller niche accelerators are typically characterized by hands-on coaching of startup teams. An additional issue is whether the accelerator's market focus will be on B2C or B2B (or a combination of both) and whether it will be oriented towards software or hardware.

3. How selective?

The answer to this question should already be obvious: accelerators by definition need to be highly selective in their startup recruitment policy, irrespective of their main goal or mission. Only startups that have the right mix of ambition, passion, and business idea sophistication should make the cut. The bar needs to be set high. Quality is decisive, distinctiveness is indispensable, and competitiveness is essential. Without exception, Silicon Valley accelerators have rigid admittance policies which they take very seriously. It would be ill-advised for accelerators on the European side of the Atlantic to set lower recruitment standards.

4. Target group: team or solo entrepreneurs?

Here, too, the answer should be quite straightforward. As almost all my interviewees emphasized, startup teams are to be preferred over solo founders. Combining all startup roles – product development, marketing, sales, customer issues, investor relations, day-to-day management, personnel hiring – into one person is bound to fail. Silicon Valley accelerators are quite outspoken in favoring balanced teams, and team assessment is consequently a standard part of the selection process. Their general experience is that successful startups are led by strong teams.

5. Cohorts or rolling admittance?

The next decision is whether to have startups participate in the new accelerator program as cohorts (over a fixed time period) or on a rolling basis. As we have seen, larger accelerators that let in substantial numbers of startups tend to be organized in terms of cohorts or batches. These startups enter the acceleration program as a class, which 'graduates' on demo day. Smaller accelerators, especially niche players, are likely to admit a limited number of startups on a continuous basis.

6. Structured program?

Related to the previous question is whether startup teams are offered a structured growth program or tailor-made coaching. Accelerator size is also critical in this case. Larger accelerators work with highly structured programs, while smaller accelerators focus on empowering individual teams. But the underlying issues that are covered in the program or coaching are, of course, highly comparable: how to create a smart, scalable, and viable business model, how to build a feasible demo, how to get traction, how to solve team challenges. Another decision that must be made is which parts of the program can be offered in-house and which parts remotely, i.e., online. The role of new communication technology can facilitate this decision. Monitoring the effectiveness of accelerator programs should also be a priority.

7. Mentorship: highly intensive or less intensive?
Every new accelerator must invest significantly in a substantial pool of committed and experienced mentors. The size of the accelerator is relevant here. In large accelerators with sizeable cohorts, mentoring tends to be less intensive (and shorter) compared to smaller niche accelerators that deliberately focus on a restricted number of startup teams. These smaller accelerators have highly intensive mentoring, with coaches working side by side with their teams in all crucial phases of startup development. Larger accelerators tend to work with mentors from outside, while smaller accelerators use internal coaches.

8. Role of investors?
One of the most important challenges for a new accelerator is creating a close network of investors that are looking for promising startups. Accelerators need to have financial resources of their own to bring promising startups to the marketplace, but they also must have a strong panel of angels and VCs willing to invest in talented startup teams and to bring scalable business ideas to the next round of funding. Accelerators that have no structural connections to investors will not last long. A fair and accountable relationship between equity percentage, investment, and accelerator program magnitude needs to be agreed upon.

9. Specialized startup support?
It is good policy for new accelerators (including accelerating platforms) to offer startups a range of support facilities such as legal advice, counseling on human resources management, ICT services, administrative expertise, and financial assistance. Silicon Valley has a strong reputation in this respect. This kind of support helps startup teams

to professionalize their new business venture and to avoid pitfalls. It also adds to the practical relevance of an accelerator's portfolio of services.

10. Culture: office space or startup vibe?
An inspiring accelerator must have the right culture to cultivate innovation, openness, sharing, entrepreneurship, and excellence – a challenging culture that is both dynamic and stimulating. Silicon Valley accelerators set an outstanding example in this respect. An accelerator or an accelerating platform is not just shared office space, not just bricks and mortar – it is much more than that. It must resonate shared dreams, shared ambitions, and shared passions. The accelerator can realize this by organizing an exciting variety of events, seminars, expert talks, pitching classes, happy hours, and dream sessions.

These ten questions incorporate the conclusions I have drawn from the experiences of accelerators based in Silicon Valley. I believe that in applying this decision tool, new accelerators in Europe will be encouraged to think in a more structured way about the precise formats that suit their mission and objectives.

Final thoughts

My study has shown that accelerators are a vital part of Silicon Valley's highly successful ecosystem. As dedicated 'schools of entrepreneurship', they help startups to develop, launch, and scale their new venture. These accelerators are in great demand by ambitious startup founding teams, also by international teams from outside the U.S. Although the metrics used to measure accelerators' success need to be further developed and validated, the impact that accelerators can have is clear. Their secret, I conclude, is that they operate as intelligent, micro-ecosystems that reinforce cultural and institutional factors that are necessary for new business acceleration such as the right mindset, the right team, and the right business idea, coupled with access to engaged mentors, investors, stakeholders, and talent and backed up by a well-functioning startup support system.

If Europe is serious about revitalizing its economic competitiveness, rejuvenating its commercial innovation performance, and elevating its entrepreneurial leadership, it must dedicate itself to investing in (for-profit and non-profit) startup accelerators. This is a joint responsibility of industrial stakeholders, innovative entrepreneurs, enterprising universities, and facilitating governments. Europe is already moving in the right direction, but much more needs to be done. One could say that the European startup agenda itself needs rapid acceleration.

Accelerators can play a distinct role in furthering European countries' ambitions to become thriving startup nations. As the Silicon Valley story shows, accelerators can make all the difference in this respect. They foster innovation, entrepreneurship, and help startups to take great ideas to the market. These are the three buzzwords that should inspire Europe in making the necessary transition to a resilient and sustainable European startup and scale-up economy that will define the 21st century. In doing so, Europe will be securing a solid economic future for itself.

Notes

1.   *The 2014 Silicon Valley index.* Joint Venture Silicon Valley/Silicon Valley Community Foundation.

2.   These and the following figures are from Ester & Maas (2016, Chapter 1).

3.   COMPASS (2015: 25).

4.   See: http://www.eu-startups.com/2016/06/top-15-europes-biggest-startup-hubs-in-2016/.

5.   *Ambitieus ondernemerschap. Een agenda voor startups en groeiers.* [Ambitious entrepreneurship. An agenda for startups and startup growth]. The Hague: Ministry of Economic Affairs, 2014.

6.   http://eur-lex.europa.eu/LexUriServ/LexUriServ.do?uri=COM:2012:0795:FIN :EN:PDF: 4.

7.   CBIA (2016) estimates that in the 1999-2013 period, the number of accelerators in the U.S. grew from 150 to 350.

8.   Nielsen (2017: 86) speaks of "startup factories".

9.   Hathaway (2016b) identified over 170 accelerators in the US between 2005 and 2015 who have collectively invested in over 5,000 startups that raised almost $19.5 billion in funding.

10.   In: Luke Deering (2014: 9), *Accelerate. Founder insights into accelerator programs.* Boulder: FG Press.

11.   See the International Business Innovation Association: https://inbia.org/.

12.   Dempwolf et al. (2014) distinguish six types of startup support organizations: incubators, venture development organizations (including social accelerators), university accelerators, proof-of-concept centers, corporate accelerators, and innovation accelerators.

13.   Graduate startup teams (N=619) were from two well-known and pioneering accelerators: Y Combinator and Techstars.

14.   See Ester & Maas (2016: 26-27).

15.   The Butler Venture Accelerator of Babson College is somewhat of an outlier even in a literal sense, as the college is located in Massachusetts. I decided to include their renowned accelerator program given the fact that Babson College is a premium university of entrepreneurship (ranking as no. 1 for 23 years) that recently expanded its program to San Francisco (www.babson. edu).

16.   According to the Seed Accelerator Rankings Project (SARP). See: http://seedrankings.com/#home.

17.   According to Entrepreneur magazine: https://www.entrepreneur.com/ article/294113.

18.   One of the Skype interviews lasted 35 minutes, due to the respondent's agenda conflicts.

19.   This applies to accelerators that provide workspace for program participants.

20. Edirol R-09, digital recording.

21. Flatworld Solutions also did the transcripts for my previous Silicon Valley book project (Peter Ester & Arne Maas, *Silicon Valley: Planet Startup*, 2016).

22. Two respondents did not reply to my repeated requests to approve their quotes.

23. This chapter is a summary of Chapters 3-10 of my book on Silicon Valley (Ester & Maas 2016).

24. Foreword to Martin Kenney (ed.) (2000), *Understanding Silicon Valley*.

25. Though terms such as "innovation ecosystems" are widely used, there is a need for conceptual clarification, consistent definition, and for prudent use of the ecosystem terminology (see Oh et al., 2016).

26. The following text is adapted from Ester & Maas (2016: 40-41).

27. Munroe (2009) adds quality of life as a discriminating factor in his Silicon Valley ecosystem model. Quality of life is undoubtedly important but its direct impact on innovation is difficult to measure other than a pull factor in attracting talent and innovative entrepreneurs.

28. Marc Andreessen, "Why software is eating the world". *Wall Street Journal*, August 10, 2011.

29. The American HBO comedy TV series *Silicon Valley* offers many examples ridiculing this "changing the world" mantra.

30. Schumpeter (1942).

31. See e.g. The Disruptive Innovation Festival (https://www.thinkdif.co/about) or the TechCrunch disrupt events (https://techcrunch.com/event-type/disrupt/).

32. For different ways in which Silicon Valley high-tech companies address innovation, see: *The culture of innovation: What makes San Francisco Bay Area companies different?* San Francisco, Bay Area Economic Institute and Booz & Company, 2012.

33. See Müller & Murmann (2016) for an alternative view.

34. http://www.entrepreneur.com/article/243660.

35. See: http://rivierapartners.com/engineering-salaries-reviewed-2/.

36. Quoted in Ester & Maas (2016: 48).

37. Hoffman & Casnocha (2012).

38. See Eesley & Miller (2012) for further data.

39. https://www.pwcmoneytree.com/Reports/FullArchive/National_2015-2.pdf.

40. *The Silicon Valley tech venture almanac*, CB Insights, New York City, 2013. Data cover the 2009-Q3 2013 period. www.cbinsights.com/research-reports/Silicon-Valley-Venture-Capital-Almanac.pdf.

41. https://www.crunchbase.com/organization/sequoia-capital#/entity (visited September 23, 2016).

42. https://www.crunchbase.com/organization/kleiner-perkins-caufield-byers#/entity (visited September 23, 2016).

43. https://www.cbinsights.com/venture-capital-silicon-valley.

44. John C. Dean, 'Fueling the revolution. Commercial Bank Financing.' In: Chong-Moon Lee et al. (eds.), *The Silicon Valley edge*, 2000: 317. The reluctance of the big commercial banks to invest in new venture startups eventually led to the creation of the Silicon Valley Bank. Dean was the bank's CEO until 2001 and is now managing general partner of Startup Capital Ventures. Banks, in the words of Stanford economist Thomas Hellmann (2000: 285), go for a financial portfolio that diversifies controllable risks. "By contrast, a venture capital firm will hold a very high-risk but high-return portfolio."

45. Bruce Booth, 'Data insight: Venture capital returns and loss rates.' *Forbes* (July 10, 2012).

46. See: https://www.cbinsights.com/blog/unicorn-overvaluation-acquisitions/, and Vivek Wadhwa, 'How crowdfunding can help save Silicon Valley from its harebrained investors.' *The Washington Post* (2016: May 12).

47. Bill Gurley, 'Above the crowd. On the road to recap: Why the unicorn financing market just became dangerous ... for all involved' (http://abovethecrowd.com/2016/04/21/on-the-road-to-recap/).

48. See for a detailed overview: Bay Area Council Economic Institute (2012). *The Bay Area innovation system. How the San Francisco Bay Area became the world's leading innovation hub and what will be necessary to secure its future.* San Francisco: Bay Area Council.

49. The latest addition to the Silicon Valley educational system is Singularity University, a private initiative focused on educating leaders to apply exponential technologies to address global change challenges (see: http://singularityu.org/).

50. The founding of Varian Associates, now Varian, is another telling example.

51. Bay Area Council Economic Institute (2014), *UC Berkeley. Stimulating entrepreneurship in the Bay Area and nationwide.* San Francisco: Bay Area Council. Figures based on the IMPLAN model, ibid., 45.

52. See: Bay Area Council Economic Institute (2016: 22).

53. http://web.stanford.edu/group/wellspring/economic.html.

54. As the Bay Area Council Economic Institute (2016: 60) concludes about the role of universities, in this case the University of California: "the university's support for entrepreneurs and startups should be not seen as a shift away from traditional academics, but as an important way to amplify their impact."

55. Bay Area Council Economic Institute (2012: 28).

56. http://facts.stanford.edu/research/.

57. See: https://techcrunch.com/2014/01/04/why-startups-hire-their-own-lawyers/.

58. Cf. http://www.huffingtonpost.com/steve-blank/silicon-valley-culture_b_963815.html.

59. "Such a conflict of interest could incentivize lawyers to take advantage of clients or fail to exercise independent judgment in advising clients due to

having an equity stake, a major downside of such arrangements for clients."
(Weinberg & Heine 2014: 61).

60. Chong-Moon Lee, William F. Miller, Marguerite Gong Hancock & Henry S.
Rowen, 'The Silicon Valley Habitat.' In: Chong-Moon Lee et al. (eds.), *The Silicon Valley Edge*, 2000: 6.

61. See: http://www.spacex.com/.

62. The way in which failure tolerance is sometimes overstressed was brilliantly ridiculed in the HBO series *Silicon Valley* where Gavin Belson, Hooli's CEO, describes failure as "pre-greatness" (Season 2, Episode 7).

63. The Silicon Valley culture of failure tolerance inspired the launching of the annual San Francisco based FailCon event ("Embracing Failure") where entrepreneurs reveal and share their business misfires and mistakes.

64. https://www.cbinsights.com/blog/startup-failure-reasons-top/ New York: CB Insights (October 7, 2014).

65. See: Gary Gereffi, Ben Rissing, AnnaLee Saxenian & Vivek Wadwha, *America's new immigrant entrepreneurs*, Duke University and Berkeley University, 2007. *American Made 2.0. How immigrant entrepreneurs continue to contribute to the US economy*. Arlington: National Foundation for American Policy, 2013.

66. Runway is running a separate EdTech accelerator as well. See chapter 5.

67. See: https://www.youtube.com/watch?v=SGJ5cZnoodY.

68. 1 square meter equals 10.76 square feet.

69. Admitted startups receive a $25,000 equity investment. Startups that relocate to Runway's San Francisco office receive up to four month of free office space for three team members.

70. For location updates, see: http://www.rocketspace.com/technology-campus-coworking-for-startups.

71. https://www.crunchbase.com/organization/credit-karma#/entity;
https://www.crunchbase.com/organization/intercom#/entity. Crunchbase does not have funding data on Twellow.

72. https://www.crunchbase.com/organization/dropbox#/entity
https://www.crunchbase.com/organization/soundhound
https://www.crunchbase.com/organization/prevedere#/entity
https://www.crunchbase.com/organization/naturebox.

73. https://www.crunchbase.com/organization/oomnitza#/entity
https://www.crunchbase.com/organization/mightyhive#/entity
https://www.crunchbase.com/organization/rigetti-computing.

74. $15.5 million according to Crunchbase:
https://www.crunchbase.com/organization/appmachine#/entity.

75. https://www.crunchbase.com/organization/life360#/entity
https://www.crunchbase.com/organization/lily-robotics#/entity.

76. https://techcrunch.com/2014/03/17/gsns-165m-bash-gaming-acquisition-nets-100x-return-for-investors/; https://www.crunchbase.com/organization/bash-gaming#/entity.

77. https://www.crunchbase.com/organization/tile#/entity.

78. https://www.crunchbase.com/organization/velocloud#/entity.

79. These four startups were acquired at undisclosed amounts and deal terms.

80. https://www.crunchbase.com/organization/valor-water-analytics#/entity
     https://www.crunchbase.com/organization/nexus-ewater#/entity
     https://www.crunchbase.com/organization/watersmart-software#/entity.

81. http://www.businesswire.com/news/home/20150615005972/en/PowWow-
     Energy-Reaps-3M-Funding.

82. https://www.crunchbase.com/organization/vartega-carbon-fiber-recycling-
     llc#/entity.

83. https://www.greentechmedia.com/articles/read/mosaic-raises-anoth-
     er-200m-for-residential-solar-loans.

84. https://www.crunchbase.com/organization/utilityapi.

85. See: http://www.usatoday.com/story/tech/news/2016/12/15/
     national-venture-capital-association-deloitte-diversity-
     survey/95453926/?utm_source=InBIA&utm_campaign=bac874acd8-
     Newsletter_March+2017_website+leads&utm_medium=email&utm_
     term=0_23a52023f9-bac874acd8-135832113.

86. https://www.crunchbase.com/organization/red-clay#/entity.

87. https://www.crunchbase.com/organization/atomwise#/entity.

88. https://www.crunchbase.com/organization/skycatch.

89. https://www.crunchbase.com/organization/pinterest#/entity.

90. http://www.rocketspace.com/technology-campus-coworking-for-startups-
     london.

91. Tweet, October 14, 2014.

92. http://www.businessinsider.com/peter-thiel-tears-into-europe-as-a-slacker-
     with-low-expectations-2014-9?international=true&r=US&IR=T.

93. Thiel (2014: 63).

94. See: https://ec.europa.eu/digital-single-market/en/startup-europe.

95. See: http://www.acceleratorassembly.eu/.

96. http://www.eu-startups.com/2016/06/top-15-europes-biggest-startup-hubs-
     in-2016/.

97. Foreword to Peter Ester & Arne Maas, *Silicon Valley: Planet Startup* (2016: 11).

98. See: 'The Dutch startup climate', keynote speech by Dutch minister Henk
     Kamp at the University of California, Berkeley, January 9, 2017.

99. http://startupdelta.org/news/Dutch-corporate-giants-pledge-to-partner-
     with-startups?mc_cid=b18fd9bcf2&mc_eid=96fa00efe8#.

100. Ibid.

101. http://www.parlementairemonitor.nl/9353000/1/j9tvgajcor7dxyk_j9vvij5ep-
     mj1ey0/vk36jula42zy?ctx=vg9pjpw5wsz1&tab=1&start_tab1=300

Glossary

Terms included in this glossary are defined within the specific context of startups and accelerators.

Accelerator metrics	Indicators that measure an accelerator's performance in growing and launching startups
Acqui-hire	Acquisition of a startup purely for its talent, not for its product or technology
AI	Artificial Intelligence. Development of intelligent machines that are able to simulate human-like thought processes
Angel investors	High net worth individuals (HNWIs), often former entrepreneurs, who privately invest in early-stage startups
AR	Augmented Reality. Real-time integration of computer-generated sensory input (e.g., sound, video, images) with the user's view of the environment
BHAG	Big Hairy Audacious Goal. Sweeping mission of a startup team to change the world
Boot camp	Intensive accelerator training event for new startup teams
Burn rate	Rate at which a startup uses up its initial capital and cash reserves
Cap table	List of a startup's securities (i.e., stock, options, warrants) and who owns those securities
Chief evangelist	Visionary ambassador and passionate promoter of a company's product and technology
Co-creation model	Accelerators that closely work with their startup teams, investors, and customers in building a new venture and preparing it for commercial take-off
Convertible note	Short-term loan that converts into equity. Often used by angel investors who wish to fund a startup without an explicit valuation
Corporate accelerator	Startup accelerator operated by a large company
Decacorn	A startup company valued at $10 billion or more (e.g., Pinterest, Palantir, Uber, Snapchat, SpaceX, Airbnb)

Deferred payments	Startups are billed only when revenues come in (e.g., by law firms)
Demo Day	Finale of accelerator program at which startups pitch their company to investors
Disruptive technology	Game-changing new technology that overturns existing markets and creates new markets
Downstream innovation	Turning new technologies and products into economic value
Ecosystem	A habitat in which all constituent elements (talent, capital, support, government, culture) are lined up in a way that they promote and sustain leading-edge innovation and pioneering entrepreneurship
Elevator pitch	Extremely concise business presentation to investors or stakeholders
Equity	Ownership interest in a startup in the form of common stock or preferred stock
Exit	Investor (often a VC) cashes in the startup investment after an IPO (Initial Public Offering) or after acquisition of the startup by a third party
'Fail Fast, Fail Often'	Silicon Valley startup mantra embracing failure as a learning experience. Values extensive experimentation, testing, early prototyping, and pivoting
Financial runway	Length of time in which a startup remains solvent until it runs out of cash
Follow-on investment right	Investor's right to startup investments in later funding rounds
FOMO	Fear of Missing Out. Anxiety among investors to be too late to invest in startups that are believed to have great potential. May lead to overinvesting
Friends, Family & Fools	Often first funders of early-stage startups
Funding series	New venture investments ranging from pre-seed to seed stage, early stage, expansion stage, to later stage. In technical terms: series Seed, series A, series B, series C, series D+

Hackathon	Hybrid of 'hack' and 'marathon'. Event at which teams of coders, engineers, and designers intensively collaborate to develop new software and new applications
H-1B visa	Allows U.S. employers to temporarily employ foreign workers in specialty occupations. Widely used in the tech industry. Under review by the Trump administration
Hockey stick growth	New venture that starts growing at a normal linear pace and at some inflection point at an exponential rate
Innovation gap	Insufficient valorization of scientific knowledge and research output into successful innovative products and services
IoT	Internet of Things. Everyday objects and devices connected to the Internet
IP	Intellectual Property, e.g., of startup inventions or technology applications
IPO	Initial Public Offering. First public sales of a startup's shares, leading to a stock market listing. Goal: new companies seeking money to expand their business
Lean startup	Business model based on continuous product iteration, measurement, and learning. Short product development cycle, lean manufacturing, and agile management
Market cap	Total market value of a startup's outstanding shares
MVP	Minimal Viable Product. Startup product with just enough features to satisfy early customers, using customer feedback for product improvements
Moonshot	Big, bold, groundbreaking project
Next Big Thing	New technology sensation that sets a global trend, is adopted by huge markets, and has a tremendous worldwide social impact
Path-dependency	Technological shifts and breakthroughs that build on preceding technologies
Pay-it-forward	Entrepreneurs 'pay back' the help they got when they started their business by offering advice and support to new entrepreneurs and startups

Permanent beta	Startup mindset: deliberately launching products that are still in the test phase. Leading business axiom: there is no such thing as a final product
Pivot	Startup strategy to redesign its initial product or service offering based on early customer feedback and market response, and sometimes to redesign the core business
ROI	Return on Investment: ratio of gain or loss of an investment relative to the amount of money invested
SaaS	Software as a Service. Cloud-based application licensed on a subscription basis
Sand Hill Road	Avenue in Menlo Park famous for its high concentration of venture capital firms. The 'Wall Street' of Silicon Valley.
Scalability	Startup product potential to multiply revenue with minimal incremental cost. A product and business model that expands to new national and international markets. This model dominates Silicon Valley's investment math
Serial entrepreneur	Entrepreneur who has founded and run several companies
Smart money	Capital consisting not only of cash investment but also of expertise, experience, mentorship, and networks. Highly valued by startup founders
'Software is eating the world'	Cherished quote by acclaimed Silicon Valley VC Marc Andreessen, indicating that established industries are invaded and disrupted by software
SoMa	South of Market Street. Trendy startup district in San Francisco
Spray and pray	Investment strategy based on high-volume startup portfolio diversification
Sweat equity	Compensation for the unpaid time and effort startup founders and team members invest in their new company in order to get it off the ground
Technology-agnostic	General accelerators that are not focused on specific technologies.
Term sheet	Bullet-point document listing the terms (funding, governance, liquidation) by which an investor will invest in a startup

'Think Big, Aim High'	Silicon Valley startup motto combining dreams, drive, and ambition
Three Comma Club	High-tech billionaires (net worth > $1,000,000,000)
Traction	Quantitative evidence of customers or users of a startup product or service
Upstream innovation	The development of new technologies and innovative products
Unicorn	Startup company with a valuation in excess of $1 billion
Valuation	Set of metrics to estimate the economic value of a startup business
Valley of Death	Feared period between first round of startup investment and steady stream of startup revenues
Valorization	Commercial and societal value-creation of fundamental research and knowledge by translating outcomes into marketable products or services
Vanity metrics	Accelerator performance statistics that look good but are not necessarily cause-effect related
VC	Venture Capital. Private equity used by firms or institutional funds to invest in potentially high-growth startups. Also: Venture Capitalist, i.e., venture capital investor
Verticals	Introduction of specific technology domains in general accelerators
Virtual accelerator program	Remote online startup team coaching and mentoring
VR	Virtual Reality. Three-dimensional computer-generated artificial environment that is designed for the user to experience and manipulate this environment as if it were the real world
Walking dead	Zombie startups that linger on too long without a realistic chance of success

References

Aaboen, Lise (2009). 'Explaining incubators using firm analogy'. *Technovation* 29, 10: 657-670.

Aerts, Kris, Paul Matthyssens & Koen Vandenbempt (2007). 'Critical role and screening of European business incubators'. *Technovation* 27, 5: 254-267.

Armour, John & Douglas Cumming (2008). 'Bankruptcy law and entrepreneurship'. *American Law and Economics Review* 10, 2: 303-350.

Barami, Homa & Stuart Evans (1995). 'Flexible recycling and high-technology entrepreneurship'. *California Management Review* 37: 33-52.

Barringer, Bruce R. & Jeffrey S. Harrison (2000). 'Walking a tightrope: Creating value through interorganizational relationships'. *Journal of Management*, 26, 3: 367-403.

Bauwen, Guy (2012). *Innovation compass. How to develop a market and build a successful business.* Puurs: ShopmyBook.

Bauwen, Guy (2013). *Growth through innovation.* Brussels: Academic and Scientific Publishers (ASP).

Bay Area Council Economic Institute (2012). *The Bay Area innovation system. How the San Francisco Bay Area became the world's leading innovation hub and what will be necessary to secure its future.* San Francisco: Bay Area Council.

Bay Area Council Economic Institute (2014a). *Reforming California public higher education for the 21st century.* White Paper. San Francisco: Bay Area Council.

Bay Area Council Economic Institute (2014b). *UC Berkeley. Stimulating entrepreneurship in the Bay Area and nationwide.* San Francisco: Bay Area Council.

Bay Area Council Economic Institute (2016). *Entrepreneurs, startups, and innovation at the University of California.* San Francisco: Bay Area Council.

Bergek, Anna & Charlotte Norrman (2008). 'Incubator best practice: A framework'. *Technovation* 28, 1-2: 20-18.

Bock, Laszlo (2015). *Work rules! Insights from inside Google that will transform how you live and lead.* London: John Murray.

Brown, John S. & Paul Duguid (2000). 'Mysteries of the region. Knowledge dynamics in Silicon Valley'. In: Lee, Chong-Moon, William F. Miller, Marguerite Gong Hancock & Henry S. Rowen (2000). *The Silicon Valley edge. A habitat for innovation and entrepreneurship.* Stanford: Stanford University Press, 16-45.

Bruneel, Johan, Tiago Ratinho, Bart Clarysse & Aard Groen (2012). 'The evolution of business incubators: Comparing demand and supply of business incubation services across different incubator generations'. *Technovation* 32, 2: 110-121.

Burns, Paul (2014). *New venture creation. A framework for entrepreneurial start-ups.* Basingstoke: Palgrave Macmillan.

California Business Incubation Alliance (2016). *California toolworks. Incubation and acceleration in the cauldron of innovation.* Santa Clara: CBIA. In collaboration with the Bay Area Council Economic Institute and Kauffman Fellows.

Castilla, Emilio J., Hokyu Hwang, Ellen Granovetter & Mark Granovetter (2000). 'Social networks in Silicon Valley'. In: Lee, Chong-Moon, William F. Miller, Marguerite Gong Hancock & Henry S. Rowen (2000). *The Silicon Valley edge. A habitat for innovation and entrepreneurship.* Stanford: Stanford University Press, 218-247.

Cerqueiro, Geraldo, María Fabiana Penas & Robert Seamans (2017). *Personal bankruptcy law and entrepreneurship.* Center for Economic Studies. U.S. Census Bureau.

Christensen, Clayton, M. (1997). *The innovator's dilemma: When new technologies cause great firms to fail*. Boston: Harvard Business School Press.

Cohan, Peter S. (2012). *Hungry startup strategy. Creating new ventures with limited resources and unlimited vision*. San Francisco: Berrett-Koehler Publishers.

Cohen, Susan G. (2013). 'What do accelerators do? Insights from incubators and angels'. *Innovations* 8, 3/4: 19-25.

Cohen, Susan G. & Yael V. Hochberg (2014). Accelerating startups: The seed accelerator phenomenon. Working paper. Available at SSRN: https://ssrn.com/abstract=2418000.

COMPASS. *The Global Startup Ecosystem Ranking 2015*. San Francisco.

Deering, Luke (2014). *Accelerate: Founder insights into accelerator programs*. Boulder: FG Press.

Dempwolf, C. Scott, Jennifer Auer & Michelle D'Ippolito (2014). *Innovation accelerators: Defining characteristics among startup assistance organizations*. Washington, D.C.: SBS Office of Advocacy.

Eesley, Charles, E. & William F. Miller (2012). *Impact: Stanford University's economic impact via innovation and leadership*. Palo Alto: Stanford University.

Ester, Peter & Arne Maas (2016). *Silicon Valley: Planet Startup. Disruptive innovation, passionate entrepreneurship & hightech startups*. Amsterdam: Amsterdam University Press.

European Commission (2013). *Entrepreneurship 2020 Action Plan*. Brussels.

European Commission (2014a). *Horizon 2020.The EU Framework Programme for Research and Innovation*. Brussels.

European Commission (2014b). *Mapping the European ICT poles of excellence: The atlas of ICT activity in Europe. European Commission*, Joint Research Centre. Report EUR 26579 EN, 2014.

European Investment Bank (2016). *Fostering innovation to remain competitive*. Luxembourg.

European Startup Initiative (2016). *Startup heatmap Europe*. Brussels: ESI.

Fan, Wei & Michelle White (2003). 'Personal bankruptcy and the level of entrepreneurial activity'. *Journal of Law and Economics*, 46: 543-68.

Fehder, Daniel C. & Yael V. Hochberg (2014). Accelerators and the regional supply of venture capital. Cambridge: Massachusetts Institute of Technology, Houston: Rice University.

Fjeldstad, Oystein D., Charles S. Snow, Raymond E. Miles & Christopher C. Lettl (2012). 'The architecture of collaboration'. *Strategic Management Journal*, 33, 6: 734-750.

Gal, Uri, Tina B. Jensen & Kalle Lyytinen (2014). 'Identity orientation, social exchange, and information technology use in interorganizational collaborations'. *Organization Science*, 25, 5: 1372-1390.

Global accelerator learning initiative (GALI) (2016). *What's working in startup acceleration. Insights from fifteen Village Capital programs*. Washington: The Aspen Institute etc.

Grimaldi, Alessandro & Rosa Grandi (2005). 'Business incubators and new venture creation: An assessment of incubating models'. *Technovation* 25, 2: 111-121.

Hallen, Benjamin L., Christopher B. Bingham & Susan Cohen (2014). 'Do accelerators accelerate? A study of venture accelerators as a path to success?'. *Academy of Management Proceedings*, Vol. 2014, 1: 12955.

Hathaway, Ian (2016a). 'What startup accelerators really do'. *Harvard Business Review*, March 1.

Hathaway, Ian (2016b). *Accelerating growth: Startup accelerator programs in the United States*. Washington, DC: The Brookings Institute.

Hellmann, Thomas (2000). 'Venture capitalists. The coaches of Silicon Valley.' In: Lee, Chong-Moon, William F. Miller, Marguerite Gong Hancock & Henry S. Rowen (eds.) (2000). *The Silicon Valley edge. A habitat for innovation and entrepreneurship.* Stanford: Stanford University Press, 276-294.

Hoffman, David L. & Nina Radojevich-Kelley (2012). 'Analysis of accelerator companies: A exploratory case study of their programs, processes, and early results.' *Small Business Institute Journal* 8, 2: 54-70.

Hoffman, Reid & Ben Casnocha (2012). *The start-up of you: Adapt to the future, invest in yourself, and transform your career.* New York: Random House.

Hunt, Vivian, Dennis Layton & Sara Prince (2015). *Diversity matters.* Mc Kinsey and Company.

Johnson, Craig J. (2000). 'Advising the new economy: The role of lawyers'. In: Lee, Chong-Moon, William F. Miller, Marguerite Gong Hancock & Henry S. Rowen (eds.) (2000). *The Silicon Valley edge. A habitat for innovation and entrepreneurship.* Stanford: Stanford University Press, 325-341.

Kamp, Henk (2017). The Dutch startup climate. Keynote speech at the University of California, Berkeley, January 9, 2017.

Katzenbach, John R. & Douglas K. Smith (1993). *The wisdom of teams: Creating the high-performance organization.* Boston: Harvard Business School Press.

Kempner, Randall (2013). 'Incubators are popping up like wildflowers ... But do they actually work?'. *Innovations* 8, 3/4: 3-6.

Kenney, Martin (Ed.) (2000). *Understanding Silicon Valley. The anatomy of an entrepreneurial region.* Stanford: Stanford University Press.

Kohler, Thomas (2016). 'Corporate accelerators: Building bridges between corporations and startups'. *Business Horizons* 59: 347-357.

Koster, Ferry. (2016). *Zelf doen is optellen, samen doen is vermenigvuldigen.* [Innovative cooperation is to multiply] Tilburg: Tilburg University Press. Inaugural lecture.

Lazear, Edward, P. (2004). 'Balanced skills and innovation'. *American Economic Review* 94, 2: 208-211.

Lebret, Hervé (2007). *Start-Up. What we may still learn from Silicon Valley.* Lausanne: Independent Publishing Platform.

Lechler, Thomas (2001). 'Social interaction: A determinant of entrepreneurial team venture success'. *Small Business Economics* 19: 262-278.

Lécuyer, Christophe (2007). *Making Silicon Valley. Innovation and the growth of high tech, 1930-1970.* Cambridge: MIT Press.

Lee, Chong-Moon, William F. Miller, Marguerite Gong Hancock & Henry S. Rowen (eds.) (2000). *The Silicon Valley edge. A habitat for innovation and entrepreneurship.* Stanford: Stanford University Press.

Lerner, Josh (2009). *Boulevard of broken dreams. Why public efforts to boost entrepreneurship and venture capital have failed – and what to do about it.* Princeton: Princeton University Press.

Leslie, Stuart, W. (2000). 'The biggest "Angel" of them all: The military and the making of Silicon Valley.' In: Martin Kenney (ed.) *Understanding Silicon Valley. The anatomy of an entrepreneurial region.* Stanford: Stanford University Press, 48-67.

Lewis, Michael (2000). *The new new thing. A Silicon Valley story.* New York: W.W. Norton & Company.

Lewis, Richard D. (2012). *When teams collide: Managing the international team successfully.* London: Nicholas Brealey Publishing.

Mazzucato, Mariana (2014). *The entrepreneurial state. Debunking public vs. private sector myths.* London: Anthem Press.

168   ACCELERATORS IN SILICON VALLEY: BUILDING SUCCESSFUL STARTUPS

Mian, Sarfraz, Wadid Lamine & Alain Fayolle (2016). 'Technology business incubation: An overview of the state of knowledge'. *Technovation* 50-51, April-May: 1-12.

Miller, Paul & Kirsten Bound (2011). *The startup factories. The rise of accelerator programmes to support new technology ventures.* London: NESTA.

Moore, Geoffrey A. (2014). *Crossing the chasm. Marketing and selling disruptive products to mainstream customers.* New York: HarperBusiness. Third Edition.

Müller, Bettina & Martin Murmann (2016). *The workforce composition of young firms and product innovation: Complementarities in their skills of founders and their early employees.* ZEW Discussion Papers, No. 16-074. Mannheim: Center for European Economic Research.

Munroe, Tapan with Mark Westwind (2009). *What makes Silicon Valley tick? The ecology of innovation at work.* Herentals: Nova Vista Publishing.

Nelson, Richard R. & Sidney G. Winter (1982). *An evolutionary theory of economic change.* Cambridge: Harvard University Press.

Nepelski, Daniel, Giuseppe Pirolo & Giuditta De Prato (2016). *European start-up hotspots: Analysis of Venture Capital financing in Europe.* Joint Research Centre, European Union, JRC Scientific and Policy Reports EUR 28021 EN, doi: 10.2791/39207.

Nielsen, Højer Nicolaj (2017). *Startup funding.* https://startupfundingbook.com/.

Oh, Deog-Seong, Fred Philips, Sehee Park & Eunghyun Lee (2016). 'Innovation ecosystems: A critical examination'. *Technovation* 54, August: 1-6.

Pauwels, Charlotte, Bart Clarysse, Mike Wright & Jonas Van Hove (2016). 'Understanding a new generation incubation model: The accelerator'. *Technovation* 50-51, April-May: 13-24.

Philips, Marc (2013). *Inside Silicon Valley. How the deals get done.* Melbourne: Melbourne Books.

Porter, Michael (1990). *The competitive advantage of nations.* New York: The Free Press.

Porter, Michael (1998). 'Clusters and the new economics of competition'. *Harvard Business Review* Nov.-Dec.: 77-90.

Public Policy Institute of California (2015). *Higher education. California's future.* San Francisco: PPIC.

Ries, Eric (2011). *The lean startup. How today's entrepreneurs use continuous innovation to create radically successful businesses.* New York: Crown Business.

Scaruffi, Piero (2014). *A history of Silicon Valley, 1900-2014.* Self-published. Silicon Valley.

Schevernels, Quintin (2016). *Suits & hoodies. Het geheim van een succesvolle start-up* [Suits & hoodies. The secret of a successful startup). Amsterdam\Antwerpen: Uitgeverij Business Contact.

Schumpeter, Joseph A. (1934). *The theory of economic development.* New York: Oxford University Press.

Schwartz, Michael & Christoph Hornych (2008). 'Specialization as a strategy for business incubators: An assessment of the Central German Multimedia Center'. *Technovation* 28, 7: 436-449.

Scillitoe, Joanne L. & Alok K. Chakrabarti (2010). 'The role of incubator interactions in assisting new ventures'. *Technovation* 30, 3: 155-167.

Senor, Dan & Paul Singer (2011). *Start-up nation. The story of Israel's economic miracle.* New York: Twelve. Hachette Book Group.

Stangler, Dana. (2013) *Path-dependent startup hubs. Comparing metropolitan performance: High-tech and ICT startup density.* Ewing Marion Kauffman Foundation.

StartupDelta: *StartupDelta Action Plan 2017.* Amsterdam: 2017. See: https://drive.google.com/file/d/0B0te96MWFu3id2dELU5FYzhHMEo/view.

Startup Genome. *Startup ecosystem report 2012*, See: http://www.venturelab.ca/The-Startup-Ecosystem-Reports-2012-and-2014.

Startup Genome. *The global startup ecosystem report 2017*. See: https://startupgenome.com/report2017/.

Startup Manifesto (2013). *Startup Europe – A manifesto for entrepreneurship and innovation to power growth in the EU* (http://startupmanifesto.eu/). Startup Europe Leaders Club.

Stross, Randall (2012). *The launch pad. Inside Y Combinator. Silicon Valley's most exclusive school for startups*. London: Portfolio Penguin.

Sturgeon, Timothy (2000). 'How Silicon Valley came to be'. In: Martin Kenney (ed.) *Understanding Silicon Valley. The anatomy of an entrepreneurial region*. Stanford: Stanford University Press, 2000: 15-47.

Suchman, Mark (2000). 'Dealmakers and counselors: Law firms as intermediaries in the development of Silicon Valley'. In: Martin Kenney (ed.) *Understanding Silicon Valley. The anatomy of an entrepreneurial region*. Stanford: Stanford University Press, 2000: 72-97.

Szycher, Michael (2015). *The guide to entrepreneurship. How to create wealth for your company and stakeholders*. Boca Raton: CRC Press.

Telefónica Europe (2013). *The accelerator and incubator ecosystem in Europe*.

Thiel, Peter (2014). *Zero to one. Notes on startups, or how to build the future*. London: Virgin Books.

Valk, de, Eva (2014). *Silicon Valley. Waar de toekomst wordt gemaakt* [Silicon Valley. Where the future is being made]. Amsterdam: Lebowski.

Vanderstraeten, Johanna & Paul Matthyssens (2012). 'Service-based differentiation strategies for business incubators: Exploring external and internal alignment'. *Technovation* 32, 12: 656-670.

Veugelers, Reinhilde (2016). 'The European Union's growing innovation divide.' Breughel Policy contribution. April 2016.

Voisey, Pam, Lynne Gornall, Paul Jones & Brychan Thomas (2006). 'The measurement of success in a business incubation project.' *Journal of Small Business and Enterprise Development* 13, 3: 454-468.

Wasserman, Noam (2012). *The founder's dilemmas. Anticipating and avoiding the pitfalls that can sink a startup*. Princeton: Princeton University Press.

Weele, van, Marijn (2016). *Unpainting the black box: Exploring mechanisms and practices of start-up incubation*. Utrecht: Utrecht University, Dissertation.

Weinberg, Alison R. & Jamie A. Heine (2014). 'Counseling the startup: How attorneys can add value to startup clients' businesses'. *Journal of Business and Securities Law*, Fall: 39-62.

Winston-Smith, Sheryl & Thomas J. Hannigan (2015). Swinging for the fences: How do top accelerators impact the trajectories of new ventures? Philadelphia: Temple University, Fox School of Business. Department of Strategic Management. Working paper.

Wise, Sean & David Valliere (2014). 'The impact on management experience on the performance of start-ups with accelerators'. *The Journal of Private Equity* 18, 1: 9-19.

Zappe, Hans (2013). 'Bridging the innovation gap'. *Nature* 501: 7468.

Appendix 1

Silicon Valley Accelerator Founders & Chief Executives
Interviewed

Saeed Amidi, Plug and Play, Sunnyvale (www.plugandplaytechcenter.com)
Sunil Bhargava, Tandem, Burlingame (www.tandemcap.com)
Gary Coover, Samsung NEXT Start, San Francisco (www.samsungnext.com)
Danielle D'Agostaro, Alchemist Accelerator, San Francisco
    (www.alchemistaccelerator.com)
Doug Davenport, Prospect Silicon Valley, San Jose (www.prospectsv.org)
Cyril Ebersweiler, HAX, San Francisco and Shenzhen (www.hax.co)
Marlon Evans, GSVlabs, Redwood City (www.gsvlabs.com)
Tom Ferguson & Nimesh Modak, Imagine H_2O, San Francisco
    (www.imagineh2o.org)
Ian Foraker, Cleantech Open, Redwood City (www.cleantechopen.org)
Brian Hoffman, StartX, Palo Alto (www.startx.com)
Ari Horie, Women's Startup Lab, Menlo Park (www.womenstartuplab.com)
Emily Kirsch, Powerhouse, Oakland (www.powerhouse.solar)
Cindy Klein-Marmer, Butler Venture Accelerator, Babson College, Babson
    Park and San Francisco (www.babson.edu)
Naomi Kokubo, Founders Space, San Francisco (www.foundersspace.com)
Duncan Logan, RocketSpace, San Francisco (www.rocketspace.com)
T.M. Ravi, The Hive, Palo Alto (www.hivedata.com)
Prashant Shah, TiE LaunchPad, Sunnyvale (www.tielaunchpad.com)
Prem Talreja, The Fabric, Mountain View (www.thefabricnet.com)
Harm TenHoff, BayLink, San Jose (www.baylink-llc.com)
Marco ten Vaanholt, BootUP, Menlo Park (www.bootupventures.com)
Matt Walters, Runway, San Francisco (www.runway.is)
Jun Wong, Hacker Dojo, Santa Clara (www.hackerdojo.com)
Elizabeth Yin, 500 Startups, Mountain View (www.500.co)

Appendix 2

Questionnaire Personal Interviews Silicon Valley
Accelerators

Name of Accelerator: Year Established:
Name of Respondent: Position:
Date of Interview: Length of Interview:

PHILOSOPHY
Q1   How did the idea of creating this accelerator originate?
Q2   Could you describe the main philosophy on which your accelerator is
     based?

USPs
Q3   What would you say are the Unique Selling Points of your accelerator?
     In what respect do you differ from other accelerators here in Silicon
     Valley or the wider Bay Area?

INTAKE/SELECTION
Q4   What are the main criteria your accelerator applies to admit or reject
     startup applicants?
Q5   What on average is your rejection rate?
Q6   How many selected applicants do you admit yearly?
Q7   Any trends in number of applicants?
Q8   Where do applicants come from? Also from outside the U.S.? If so,
     which countries?
Q9   Do you focus on solo startup founders or on teams? Does it matter?
Q10 What is the percentage of program dropouts? What are the main
     dropout reasons?

FOCUS
Q11 Is your accelerator focused on particular technologies or more general?
Q12 Do you focus on certain target groups of startup founders?
Q13 Who are your main competitors?

FUNDING

Q14   Is your accelerator backed by an investment fund?

Q15   Do participating startups have to pay a fee? If so, how much?

Q16   Does your accelerator take equity in participating startups, and if so how much?

Q17   If not, why not?

Q18   What are the main ingredients of your accelerator's business model?

PROGRAM

Q19   What are the basics of your accelerator program?

Q20   One program or several programs?

Q21   How long is the program?

Q22   How would you rate the program's intensiveness?

Q23   What are the main program milestones

Q24   How is mentoring organized? How do you select mentors?

Q25   Any role for strengthening participants' entrepreneurial & managerial skills?

Q26   Is it promoted that startup teams work together? If so, how?

Q27   How are VCs involved? How is access to startup funding organized?

Q28   What about access to lawyers and accountants?

Q29   How is networking organized in the program?

Q30   How do you create a dynamic startup vibe and passionate accelerator culture?

Q31   Did the program substantially change in the last few years; if so why?

CHALLENGES

Q32   What are the main challenges your accelerator is facing?

COOPERATION

Q33   What are the main external partners or organizations here in Silicon Valley or the wider Bay Area that your accelerator works with?

Q34   Do you have structural relationships with universities or research labs in Silicon Valley or the Bay Area?

SUCCESSES

Q35 What are the most successful startups that participated in your accelerator program?

Q36 Why do you think they are successful?

Q37 What in your experience are the main success and fail factors of startups after they completed your program?

Q38 Which startup that completed your program are you most proud of and why?

Q39 Do you monitor your participants after they completed the program?

Q40 How much overall has been invested by external funds in your startups?

FINAL QUESTIONS ON FUTURE

Q41 Do you plan any changes in the setup or the program of your accelerator?

Q42 Any plans to go to Europe?

Thank you very much for your time. We truly appreciate your cooperation.